ROUGHY

Fishing the Mid-Ocean Ridges

ROUGHY

Fishing the Mid-Ocean Ridges

Alistair [A.J.] Peach

BACH BOOKS

Available from Amazon.com, CreateSpace.com, and other
retail outlets

Published 2015
Bach Books
Extemporary1@gmail.com
A catalogue record for this book is available
from the National Library of New Zealand

For Greg Keen, Kenny, Cricket, Cossie & Logger

Special thanks to Rick Wilkinson, Gusta Peach, Davey Cleary,
Paul Hendry, Chris Cowan,
Sva Brooke-White, Barbara Polly, Blair Polly,
Flash McBride, Eddie Stockley, Lynette Archer.

ISBN   978-0-473-25757-6

Contents

Charts and Fish Photos

Charts

Fish

Boat Photos & Other Bits

Fishing Vessels

Drawings - Details & Other Bits

Preface

§

As a warning and an aside –
I am a serial confabulator and stories once told with precise accuracy habitually inherit embellishments in double quick time.

Small [and large] coastal hamlets have, at various times gone into uproar because of my exaggerations. It has been a harmless character fault of mine since childhood and an involuntary habit that not only secured my reputation and earned me many dear friends but it gained me just as many detractors.

Friends will listen and wait for the exaggeration and then stop me with a disbelieving interjection. I embrace this interruption. I instinctively respond to their scoffing with an even more preposterous opinion [or fact], often so outrageous it can cause a guffaw.

I have no excuse for this impulsive behaviour. It can probably be attributed to some instability, my mother, or the fisherman in me [if an excuse is necessary].

This story, in spite of heavy-handed editing and my battles with truth and self, still contains some over-descriptions, some of which do very little for the story.

It is a fishing yarn for Kenny Rand and Chris [Cricket] Lind, who sadly drowned on the Greymouth bar. It is also for Cossie, Logger and others who liked a yarn.

This yarn [and memoir], is about a decade of fishing that began in the south of New Zealand at Jackson Bay

From Jackson Bay, a fishing hamlet, [which Glover called 'the terminus of the sea'] where we rowed to our moored vessels to start a fishing trip; the story progresses to the major New Zealand ports, where skills were needed to deal with uniformed gate guards. It is a story about fishing the mid-ocean ridges and the Louisville Ridge in particular.

The chapters chronicle the progress of my lifelong fishing co-dependant Michael [Surge] Buskin and his struggles to obtain fishing quota to provide a retirement income.

My hope is to produce a book which can stand in a bookshelf, 'spine-to-spine and head to head', competing with Bert Fisher's underground and underwater trilogy, Divers of Arakam.[1]

Wherever possible I've tried to name the people who were part of the story, - the true witnesses, although if you check with them, they are likely to chorus [with fortissimo] 'No! that's not what happened'.

Typically, each event has a different version and all versions are likely to change with the passage of time.

When I told my lawyer I was going to write a book about fishing `Deep Sea` - he eyed me and said bluntly, "Say nothing about cabin boys," then he added with a shark-like smile, "That's free legal advice AJ."

---

[1] .Bert Fisher died 2007.

THE BEGINNINGS o o o o

1...Surge and the Congers

South Island - June [1993] ○ ○ ○ ○

My fishing life went on hold. I got 'grounded' by a head-on traffic accident. The impact imploded my car, leaving a crash site that the local police [Murchison] report stated was a 'large amount of debris.' It was a fair description, but when recalling the details of the crippling accident, I preferred to describe it as, `a sea of bondi-fill and shattered safety-glass.' Panel-filler chunks at accident sites were a common sight in those days. When I surveyed the scene through the stars in my traumatised eyes, it looked like the bird-shit at a vacated shag-roostery.

I'd bought the old V8 car from sphagnum moss-pickers; they had used it in the Westland wetlands and they had bogged it up [big] with body filler. After my purchase, the car went from the dank air of swamps to the salt-laden air of a harbour-side and although I thoroughly anointed the panels in fish oil [inside and out], it kept rusting and needing filler.

A tourist caused the collision. The culprit was a German air-traffic controller, who obviously wasn't observing his '*safe separation standards*' and his avoidance systems had gone haywire. He was touring the South Island with his family, after a stint of strike-breaking at American airports and he was driving on the wrong side of the road.

At the time of the accident, I was returning to the West Coast from Nelson to fish a winter season. The car radio had Louis Armstrong singing `*What a Wonderful World*` when the

1

sightseer drove into me! After the police paperwork was completed, I was driven back to *'whence I`d come'* in an ambulance. If I`d known the ambulance trip back to Nelson would be a step to fish the Louisville Ridge, 'I would`ve felt no pain.'

At first, I thought it ironic that a controller of traffic could get it so wrong. Then I started thinking the full game theory of conspiracy. After the accident it seemed everyone I knew [or met] had been affected by a tourist accident, even the CEO of the hospital had been maimed by one. My conspiracy theories focused on the rental car companies, the Transport Department, and their actuaries who knew the truth about who was paying the price. Mulling over conspiracy theories can relieve a lot of pain.

The accident broke my ribs and the steering wheel cut up my face leaving a cleft lip that wouldn't hold beer froth. The ACC doctor called the wound *'subsidiary disfigurement'*. I checked a dictionary and it seemed like a valid description. I`d lived a careless and carefree lifestyle and I already had facial scars, a deformed nose and a fat ear to show for it.

A month later, outside the Nelson courthouse, the German family apologized [repeatedly] and they did it sincerely. It probably helped them but it did little for me. If I`d known then the courthouse corridors would be a step to fish the Louisville Ridge, I would have been a bit more accepting.

Recuperation - Nelson [1993] ₒ ₒ ₒ ₒ

In June 1993, I was experiencing a restless recuperation. I was suffering pain from broken ribs and a mouth full of stitches. It was a time of major irritability but I fought the irritably by thinking of ways to stop foreign tourists from driving like they were at home. I fought the pain by brooding over conspiracy theories.

Keeping my face still and not talking stopped the stitch ends from stabbing my tongue and inner mouth. Not talking was pain free but difficult because I'm talkative. I've been called a waffler, and worse, in my time. It was a situation with a mantra, *'Don't grin just bear it'*.

I reasoned my recuperation would be helped if I utilized healthy obsessions and I decided to study fish while I healed. Surge sent me a banana-box full of fish publications from his *'clutter'*. The books were glossy, some were very extensive encyclopaedias, others were classics, and the collection was sized to suit a long recuperation.

Surge ₀₀₀₀

Surge [Mike Buskin] and I met playing midget rugby when we were a side-line ballboy team for the seniors. We grew up living three bays apart on a rocky coastline and we went on fishing trips in our pre-teen years [encouraged by our parents]. We were both freckled and lonely-types [sans siblings] and we have shared dreams with an uncomplicated friendship ever since.

Surge and I talk fish and our conversations mostly start with "Why don't we......."

Fish books fill the voids of Surges house. He calls his collection *'the clutter'* but to a casual visitor it would be borderline hoarding.

He dreams of working a small inshore fishery into his old age, and via a lengthy elimination process, he had decided to become a Conger eel catcher and he expected me to support him. Over the years he'd explored a variety of fisheries.

He had tried to catch Octopus using an old Mediterranean method which relied on curiosity, a marble rock; and a drain-pipe. We talked it up but it was a failure.

He had tried catching Blind Eels [Lamprey], using no-cost

rotten bait and broken bait bags, but we couldn't sustain a pub presence with the catch earnings!

Surge obstinately pursues his dreams and he often has trouble recognizing a lost cause.

***

I started the fish studies with Abysmal Snailfish – *a fish whose males have been found with incubating ova in their mouths.* There were over three hundred fish starting with A and I starting to feel task tiredness before B.

It was low point in my recovery. I had depression [with pain], and I was constantly wrestling with my mental state to stay positive. I needed a change of luck [and focus] and my friends [Soozie and Shane] rescued me. Their help resulted in a fishing job on a boat catching Orange Roughy at the Challenger Plateau. The vessel wouldn't be ready for six months, leaving time for me to recuperate. The job offer perked me up and if I sat motionless, my broken ribs didn't hurt. When my mouth stitches were extracted, I was back on solids and reading about fish with enthusiasm from '*b to zee*'.

I sailed into the B's, beginning with Baabundyi, `*a fish that inhabits coral-reef moats*`. It's called the Unicorn Fish in most English speaking places [and it's the first fish photographed when someone gets a new underwater camera in the tropics].

I got to C and my progress slowed to paua-pace at Cod, after one hundred and sixty varieties starting at Cable Cod, I gave up. I met my Waterloo at Rusty-Red Cod. Cod easily deflate a good bout of fish obsession, but then, beyond Cockle-bullies and Cod there's Conger eels to contemplate.

A few years before, Marijo, a Queensland skipper we worked for had revealed Conger eels were a delicacy in France. Surge and I thought the word delicacy [*dally-kay-ceee*] sounded good in his Dalmatian accent.

Marijo's statement had spawned our initial interest and it fuelled a fire of inquisitiveness. Both of us had memories of how Congers turned up in the crayfish pots when we were crewing on a crayfish-boat in South Westland. There, the northerly blows made the Congers bite hard and dealing with them made for a long day. In those days we chunked the congers for crayfish holding bait, even though, it was bait that never started any feeding frenzies. You couldn't help thinking there was a better use for Conger flesh and Marijos '*dally-kay-ceee*' comment pointed to possibilities.

Chris Fouhy and a good sized conger eel
Cover Photo: [*Jim O`Brien*]   '*A Red Cod and a Conger Eel.*'

Books from the National Library Service, a primitive internet search and interrogating fishing friends reinforced Marijo's opinion. Another important fact [for us] was that Congers lived well in captivity. Surge and I can get obsessive when a fish lingers on in our minds. We were forever asking Conger questions.

The local fishing company manager [Biggsy] looked suspicious when we questioned him about Congers, but his reply was encouraging. "There's a bit of a market. It comes and goes." His answer was what we wanted to hear, and we repeated, `bit of a market, it comes and goes` to each other for a day or two.

We began investigating the transport details for a catch with a Singaporean tropical fish exporter. A lawyer friend, working in Marseilles, arranged a buyer for shipments which would be worth $us10K. Our wallets seemed to swell and pressure our pockets when we thought about it. Our friends were split. Some said "You are on to something," and others said "Why do you want to catch those bastards?"

Sue [Surges` second wife] called us *'mission-junkies'* and she was probably right. We were blinkered in the pursuit of fishing our retirement years. We talk fishing; it is our bond. Fishing talk tickles our minds with its unknowns and thoughts of success, and even notoriety. Both of us had been in and out of the fishing industry and had realistic expectations, but they don`t stop us dreaming. None of it mattered at the time. The only thing we were interested in was the next step in the conger project.

Surge made a conger-catching trap modelled on a Hinaki whararua eel-pot. He floated it to hold it a half-a-metre off the sea floor to eliminate a crayfish by-catch. He studied wicker weaving and loved the phrase *'French-randing'*.

He was badly slashed by *bush-lawyer* getting a load of *supple-jack* to make the trap and his wounds made for a good bush story, which he retold without prompting [too many times].

The eel-entrance to the pot had a lazy-gooseneck to stop a diving-bird by-catch. There was a foil [like a wind vanes tail] to point the trap into the current and the bait-bag was a perforated Milo tin filled with dog food. He kidded that the real traps would be carbon-fibre and we habitually spent late nights discussing the future of the Conger fishery.

We applied to the Ministry of Fisheries for an exploratory permit for our *Conger incarcerators* [or CI's], as we had started to call them]. Trap CI.v1 was tested north of Greymouth by the large rock stacks at Moutukiekie [once the Twelve Mile] and it caught three good-sized Congers in two fathoms of water.

We fished from dusk to dawn on the Tasman Sea's hard-edge, in 'trap testing country'. The terrace mussel-beds supplied bait and a sure footing while we bobbed for crayfish and cast baited hand-lines over the steep edges.

The catch was cooked over a smelly, smoky fire fuelled with damp driftwood and bits of crumbly coal from the high tide tiers. It was a lip-smacking, primal-food adventure.

The long night and thick smoke made us delirious. We felt like we had proved a point together and we shared a crayfish which is always special. The testing night was very cold, but it didn't matter.

When we drove back to Surge's house in the morning, we saw a spectacular sea-smoke and beach-foam display north of Rapahoe. The sea-smoke and foam billowed, playing with the air mass and our minds. Rock rubble beaches are softer than the whitest sand when sea smoke comes alive.

It was a special moment [smoke, foam, and delirium] and we decided our trap testing was complete. We were capable of procrastination and the trap testing could have lasted years without the beach-foam moment. We had a Conger catcher which was going to give us a stake in this untapped fishery, or at least, provide some income and save us from having to drink home-brew into our twilight years.

Our top-secret [*hush-hush*] Conger catcher [CI.v1] was stored in Surge's shed. We hung it from the roof timbers and watched, as it became a source of curiosity for mason bees. Surge had fifty acres of Pakahi country, out the back of Atarau [up the Grey River] which he loved with a passion for its low maintenance. Without prompting, he would kick-start himself into a rave about why he lived where he lived. "The only post on the property holds up the mail box; the dirt's solid as concrete a millimetre down and nothing grows no weeds, no grass, just moss and severely stunted scrub."

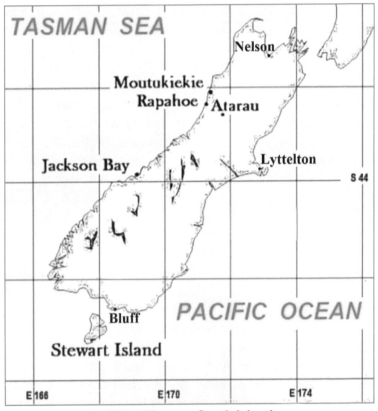

Story Places ~ South Island

After saying that he always ended with, '*there's plenty of trout in the river too*'. It was odd statement, because Surge didn't like trout fishing. He was a saltwater fisherman, [he didn't even like whitebaiting]. He had earned his nickname by out-fishing everyone at the coastal surge-ponds and sea-spouts.

"When you hook a fish in the surge, its skin is bright and its taste kapai." Surge would go on and on, he loved to talk about the dangers and thrills of rocky coast fishing, it was his pet subject. He could talk rock fishing all day, even standing in the rain '*in a pahka on the Pakahi*'.

The Conger project 'business plan' had been priced realistically and it was easy to visualize the whole operation.

Live Congers to Paris for bouillabaisse or to Honolulu for luaus or Tauranga for tangis. The possibilities were endless...

... '*Live Conger Eels fresh packed in prime Bull Kelp [Bladder Kelp $1 extra].a fishing dream never ends.*

Conger Costings

7 metre aluminium pontoon boat	28,500
Outboard engine	14,700
30 x conger incarcerators	15,000
3 x conger transporters	15,000
1 x conger holding pot	3,000
Ropes, floats, anchors	2,500
Fees & legal	5,000
	$ 83,700

Call it ninety grand max, we'd reckoned and resolved it at thirty grand each with the rest from the bank.

Surge asked wife Sue if she would back him and she said, "Just leave me out of it. Your scheme to export Parrotfish to German aquariums was where I got off the bus."

He winked at me calling her '*adventures great wheel-clamp.* '

Inwardly Sue laughed but outwardly she kind-of smiled and he called it approval. Sue wasn't keen on his fishing schemes. The schemes caused long separations and wasted money that should have been spent on the house, [which wasn't finished, despite a twenty-year construction effort] but she never tried to change him.

The bank enquired, "Do you have Quota?"

At the time, a FIN [Fisher Identification Number] was needed to commercially fish a species. Quota was needed for a FIN. We explained we were trying to establish a catch history so we would be eligible for quota, but the banker said we didn't have a solid enough financial base. It's well known banks don't understand any primary industry and the fishing business in particular. They turned down our loan application, which delayed the project, but we knew we were onto a winner. The costs didn't deter us – costs don't discourage mission junkies.

We would have to buy some finfish Quota to get a FIN number and call the Congers by-catch.

Conger Eels from 'The Clutter' ₀ ₀ ₀ ₀

Tuna

Maori legend tells the story of how Maui killed the water creature called Tuna in revenge for having seduced his wife, Hine, while she was bathing. According to the legend, Maui dug a trench and placed skins in it as bait. Then when Tuna made his way into the trench, Maui chopped him into bits. The different pieces of Tuna then became other beings.

The head went to the rivers and streams and became freshwater eels who also took the name Tuna: the tail reached the ocean and became the Conger Eels: the long hair-like nostrils on the tip of his upper jaw turned into vines and other plants: and his blood coloured the wood of the Rimu and Totara trees.

The Southern Conger Eel

Conger eel [Conger verreauxi], our largest and most common marine eel, is an under-rated fish. Its rich, firm white flesh is excellent for braising, roasting, smoking, in fish stews and in soups. The common Conger eel of New Zealand is almost identical to the species regarded highly in other countries, for example in France where it is often used in bouillabaisse and in Chile where it is used in a soup which is a national dish. These eels grow to 2m long and yield large firm blocks or fillets of very white flesh.

A Brief Conger Dissertation ₒ ₒ ₒ ₒ

The further south you go the bigger the Conger. They are mostly shoulder height to the deck long. When held up by the gills and the slippery bustards weigh as much as a bag of cement. Man-size is the only way to describe the Southern Congers, although the politically correct would prefer 'jumbo'.

Congers are mean mouthed and a hit from a flaying tail is the equal of a horse kick, making them business at both ends.

They'll try to latch on to anything and when they succeed, they do furious crocodile rolls with their teeth barbed in. The monsters, given a chance, can grab onto the end of leggings, and spin resulting in a ligature that shuts off the blood supply to your feet with a crippling effect. When Congers haven't got a mouthful of mischief they have a mind alerting bark.

Anyone who has worked the deck of an inshore fishing-boat or had much to do with them develops ways of dealing with the creatures, normally this involves some surgery with a large-knife, and *cabbage knife* size is best.

A deep cut across the back of the eel, anywhere between the back of the head and the anal-sphincter [*as a boffin sez*], severs their spinal-cord and quietens them down no end. The all-weather skills needed to do this on a pitching deck, without fuss, develop quickly when you crayfish for a living.

Normally the eels are dealt with in the cray pots with the blade slipped between the steel-mesh skin of the pot and used like a guillotine, but often they have to be dealt to on the deck because their thrashing around is damaging the catch in the pots.

Don't get it wrong 99.99% are released unharmed but one in a thousand dies with a story.

The occasions when overkill knife-action severs an eel in two, you are likely to see the head of the Conger take a large mouthful of its own detached tail section [ouroboros-like]. They are driven to latch their powerful jaws onto something, even in death.

When I was working winter scallops around the Great Barrier Reef of Oz, I had no fear, or trouble, dealing with sea snakes, a dozen at a time, because of the skills learnt during my years handling Conger eels while cray fishing.

Dealing with one difficult Conger is a life experience the equal of landing any big fish. Anyone who has dealt with Congers will readily tell you a story to back this up and people who have dealt with them in small boats will relive a nightmare or two.

THE CHALLENGER PLATEAU....

2...Newfies & Bellows Fish

Wellington - Christmas [1993] ○ ○ ○ ○

Friends in Nelson introduced me to a contact and the meeting resulted in a job on the sixty-four metre deep-sea trawler *Newfoundland Lynx.*

The Lynx was at sea, on its shakedown trip and I was part of the half-crew rostered off, at the start of a two trips on and one off rotation. My ribs had healed and I was off to sea on a big trawler. I was excited beyond exaggeration and the elation had me singing sea shanties, [and I felt like dancing a jig].

A dozen of us were waiting shore-side for the Lynx to dock and management held us captive at the dockside. Waiting for boats tests patience. It is a time for careful budgeting, although few people around a fishing vessel are capable of following a budget, including management.

I was in my forties and had been commercial fishing for twelve years. You tend to earn an A+ for financial juggling after ten years of being caught short at the wharf. The *Lynx* would dock in Wellington after its sea trials.

Wharf waiting is a time when you value friendships the most and I re-united with Wellington friends who I hadn't seen for over ten years. Sarah, Dianne, and I had gone to a standout exhibition of Tony Fomisons works. Linda and I spent hours talking about the past. Geoff and I talked bits of recovered memory and alcohol recovery. I had sessions with Rex solving cryptic crosswords in Crunch`s bar, and old flames were rekindled. It was a life of social excess for a fisherman like me, and when I was away from it, I was in the new city library, researching Conger eels using the new electronic database.

While we waited for the vessel to return to port rumours started going around wharf-side bars and slipways that the vessel was a lemon and the fish stocks were gone. All the news filtering back from the boat was gloomy and it propelled the waiting crew to drink, and a broke status. This progressed to begging and then bludging off friends [and strangers].

Then the first officer reported there was, "Bilge level Ponzischeming afoot using ill-gotten *Time Out* tickets". But, as always, there's no setback a high interest loan won`t fix and we immersed ourselves in debt.

When the vessel did dock, there were boarding parties of winch and electronic technicians. A stalemate developed with no access codes to the winch computer system. The computer system was capable of simulating trawls and it could do self-diagnosis but the menu was code guarded.

The `just docked and paid up crew` provided buddy and mate loans rescuing a poverty situation for those waiting to sail.

Finally, a technician was found in Norway but when he arrived, he insisted on doing an overdue service of the winches. The service created more delays and we waited for parts, kits and seals to arrive. Winch repairs and electronic fixes are a handbrake in any fishing operation. We waited at the wharf like hundreds before us, but I was still too excited to care. We were off to fish the middle of the Tasman Sea and that meant adventure.

Each time it appeared we were ready for departure, the engineers, [who were getting a lot of stick], would report another failure of some mechanical fitting or fixture and the pilot was deferred numerous times. It annoyed the Port Authorities to the point of non-co-operation and the boat was listed without an ETD.

Further delays prompted the crew to the food complaint stage of unhappiness. They had been forced by the delays to live aboard and do mundane tasks [unpaid] to keep themselves occupied and out of the police cells. Anxiety with no grog usually makes a crew disorderly and food complaints are the first steps to unruliness.

More delays meant the high interest rate loans were starting to be called in by insecure loan sharks. We would receive retainers ranging from 150/250 dollars a day when our contracts were signed. The fishing company got the crew wharf-side early and left the signing of contracts until the last moment before sailing. Every port in the world has a bit of 'short-changing' going on.

Small advances against catch bonuses stopped the credit card company calls, but the crews' wives and girlfriends still rang all day long hoping for a departure date and the chance of some monetary relief to run their households.

The Lynx - [1994] ○ ○ ○ ○

**Newfoundland Lynx [Built as Nororn in Norway]   LOA 54 m
Photo 1987 Bremerhaven after extension to 64 m 1297 GT**

The Newfoundland Lynx's shakedown trip was a disaster and is now known around the coast, [by those who were there, and few who weren't], as the '*crossed door tour of ninety-four.*'

The doors cross after the net becomes fast, and when the gear is hauled back, one door comes free before the other. The doors need the pressure from the net gear to maintain their aspect. A loose door doesn't have that advantage, and it becomes an uncontrollable flyer. In 1994, the *Lynx* door crossovers had been caused by computer problems. The computer had been designed to recognize a loose door but it didn't happen on trip 1 1994. [A pitted 5mm ball bearing, which controlled hydraulic pressures, got the blame].

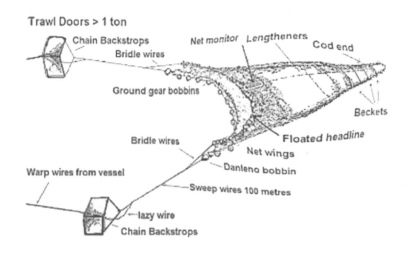

TRAWL PARTS

Crossed doors are a nightmare in rough seas as well as a major problem for the deck crew and winch drivers. Fixing the situation requires the untwisting and un-knitting of two one-tonne [and larger] doors with their heavy chain and wire attachments. The trawl-doors can get themselves into unimaginable tangles and usually, a gas-cutting torch, and the call *'put a gilsen around it!'* is needed in the fix.

***

The Lynx was a Norwegian built factory trawler. It was named *Nororn* when it was launched and it fished the North Sea before going to St Johns, Newfoundland. There it was renamed *Newfoundland Lynx* [she had sister ships] and operated as a tax advantage for a celebrity sportsman.

Vessels, like the Lynx, were `*Ice Class*`. They could bust their way into frozen Artic seas and trawl beneath the ice. The ice barrier [which had acted like a fish bunker-cover for eons], had become little more than a petty obstruction to the engineering of the *Lynx*. If problems were encountered, Joe (Blow) would drawl dismissively *"Ya jus` cawled an icebreaker"*.

These trawlers were designed to catch shrimp off the sea floor and the fish at refuge, under the ice sheets. The result of taking these two very serious bites at the food chain with too many of these up-to-the-minute vessels was a classic case of *overfishing* and it affected the whole of the Grand Banks in the North Atlantic.

The Lynx became a Roughy hunter in 1994. It was bought by a small listed fishing-company who purchased it, along with another smaller vessel, for a price equal to the cost of a new computer system running the Lynx`s winches. The computer system kept the trawl wires tensioned evenly and consequently the net trawled square and worked at its maximum efficiency.

The trawl-deck had port and starboard sets of sweep drums allowing the fishing master to have the choice of two different nets set up ready for fishing. Those nets could have different cod-ends, bobbin-rigs, and sweep configurations for fishing different terrains.

The vessel was showing its age and a lack of maintenance

when it had arrived in NZ. "Pretty boats don't catch more fish" said one of the owners who obviously wasn't into rust-removal or painting.

The *Lynx's* skipper was Reg [Stevens], a veteran roughy hunter regarded by most as 'the master'. He was affectionately known as the A.A.O.E [Absolute Authority on Everything] to some and as the Witchdoctor to others. It had been said he could catch Orange Roughy down a dunny if only he could work out a way of getting the net down there.

One thing is certain about Reg, nobody has ever been able to catch as many factory-friendly 'hundred-tonne' bags of Roughy with his regularity. He was a leader in the push to find new fisheries and his success came from mapping new fishing areas using police crime-scene thoroughness. His fishing methods, although well known, are rarely copied. His methods however are often subjected to shortcuts by others, which is a thing that would both annoy and amuse him.

Reg had Pacific ancestry and his birthplace was rumoured as anywhere from Te Wae Wae Bay to Ratu-land. His concern for the Pacific took him to Moruroa [Aopuni] on the yacht *Free,* when the French were carrying out their atomic testing.

The enthusiasm of Dave [Cunliffe] had pushed the Lynx enterprise to fruition. Dave had graduated through the fishery via the Nelson Sealord and Sanford vessels. Dave and Reg had meticulously planned every aspect of the venture. Like grandmaster chess players, they had strategies for every contingency [and all of Murphy's laws]. The Lynx was chosen from a pool of sixty fishing boats that were '*on sale*' in Newfoundland.

. Reg and Dave were joined by another Dave [Hoy] and the three of them chose a crew from their earlier vessels and filled the gaps with the unattached patrons of the Customhouse Hotel, [Nelson] including the barman [Butch].

The vessel came to New Zealand with *Newfies*. Newfoundland fishers: Captain Joe, bosun Billy and Chief engineer Bernie had travelled with the vessel and they could talk at length [and with humour], about chipping ice and gutting cod.

Some of our crew were from the Chatham Islands and they would talk at length [and with humour], about eating Albatross, Wekas, Crayfish and Cod. The two groups from frontier-lands, poles apart, played a complicated card game called *forte-fives* and they enjoyed each other's company.

1994 was near the culmination of New Zealand's fishing expansion. For fishermen like me, the expansion had caused a shift from coastal *forty footers* to forty metre and larger deep-sea trawlers. The demand for New Zealand's fish on the world markets had been the main catalyst for the expansion and in turn, it led to larger vessels. The inshore crews shifted, lured by the chance of a steady pay on the large all weather boats.

Greek soldier [Hoplite] and fishy namesake [Hoplostethus]

A bit about Orange Roughy ○ ○ ○ ○

Roughy was known since 1889 as Hoplostethus Atlanticus. It was named after the heavily armoured Greek foot soldiers of a bygone era. Roughy is a member of the Trachichthyidae family [slime heads], and *slime head* was not a marketable name. It was first found in commercial quantities in Cook Strait in 1957 and given its name by the New Zealand Governor General [Reeves] and it caused rapid changes to the offshore fisheries.

History recalls the Shinko Maru caught a bag of Roughy in 1975, but it didn't create any interest, because the foreign consultant called it *'diarrhoea fish'* [the black stomach lining of the fish causes the liquid discharge].

There was speculation the large European factory trawlers had been harvesting the species from the flat areas, in deep waters for some time. Orange Roughy was marketed worldwide as `deep-sea sea-perch`. Various foreign owned vessels have laid claim to starting the Orange Roughy industry – Professor Buguoki, Kalatan, and Wesermunda are mentioned in publications.

In 1985, Roughy was being caught on the steep edges of Cook Strait. The boats catching it were former North Sea trawlers, *Seafire, Galliard*, and *The Buccaneer*. These boats had arrived in the country with nets that were soon redesigned and attached to newly developed ground gear.

Kiwi skippers and net makers started experimenting. The biggest advances happened when net monitors started showing net ground-ropes relative to the bottom and gave temperature readouts. The temperature read outs meant the nets` depth could be calculated from the *"environmental [or adiabatic] lapse rate."*[1]

The Cook Strait edges led the way to new fishing grounds on New Zealand's continental shelf margins, then to the high ground in international waters outside New Zealand's 200 nautical miles Exclusive Economic Zone. Kiwis went deep-sea fishing, stretching the reach of the NZ`s deep-sea trawler fleet

---

[1] Temperature decreases uniformly for every 100m of change in air or sea

to over 1200 miles each side of the country.

New Zealand Roughy fishing ideas developed at a period when fishing technology was making rapid advances. These days you will find Kiwi Roughy fishermen worldwide using technology developed for moon mapping and advanced warfare.

Trawling nets down underwater mountains after difficult peak-top landings, using 2000 metres of wire, takes a degree of nerve. The trawling is done in any sea [up to sixty knots and six-metre swells], using a fishing trawler handed down from some other unrelated fishery. The rewards can be high but mistakes are expensive and they can terminate a skipper's career.

A bit about the Challenger Grounds o o o o

In 1992 four NZ vessels and one from Australia, targeting Roughy, worked the Challenger Plateau and landed almost 1500 tonnes of catch. In 1993, a major effort by 30 boats produced over 5000 tonnes. These figures together with a supply of cheap boats from the collapse of the Grand Banks fishery in the North Atlantic triggered the investment in our vessel by the company Seafresh.

The Bellona Trough separates the Lord Howe Rise from the Challenger Plateau and together they buttress the submarine forces of the Tasman Sea from New Caledonia to the Southern Alps of NZ. Some people believe Russian and Japanese trawlers had been fishing the flat areas in these waters since the fifties. It is certainly a possibility. The Norwegians were there with the vessel *Longva* and a few NZ crew in 1993. What began as a winter Roughy fishery became a year round venture by 1994.

The Bellona Trough was named after the HMNZS Bellona [Dido design] which surveyed the area in 1952 after surviving an attack from an Australian warship - radio interference got the blame.

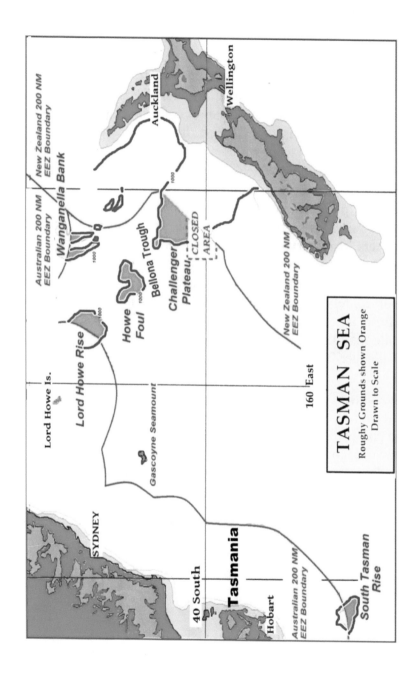

Wellington - Late February [1994] ○ ○ ○ ○

The ongoing anxieties caused by the delays slowly eased. Everyone on board went about their sea jobs when we cast off and a good atmosphere took over the vessel.

The ceremony of embarkation could be seen everywhere. Deck hands were wearing clean overalls and using chinstraps on their helmets as they fleeted the heavy hawse lines with synchronicity and teamwork.

The engine-room watch-keepers went through their routine checks. Their radio communications with the bridge used textbook pronunciations and classic phonetic emphasis. In the wheelhouse, the officers were making small talk on safe subjects. On everyone's mind were debts and the size of the catch needed to pay them off.

Dale [the mate] had hoisted the '*H for hotel*' flag and the pilot politely ordered precise courses and pitch settings. The helmsman repeated the courses and reported the vessel's speed while the mate made cups of tea to order. We were off to the Challenger Plateau.

Thoughts of instant and overwhelming success were shattered that year at the Challenger. In spite of scouring the grounds to the point where a needle would have been 'de-haystacked', the spawn aggregation eluded us and we returned to port with a hundred tonnes of frozen, head off and gutted Cardinal, a troublesome water maker and a broken framo pump.

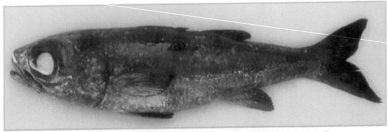

Cardinalfish [Photo P.N.Duartel DOP Azores]

Cardinals are a deep-water fish down to 600m. They are known to fisherman as *'flies'* because of their eyes but they have some commercial demand.

We had two water makers, one was a distillation machine that relied on a venturi vacuum and the engine exhaust for its operation, and the other was a reverse osmosis desalinator which used sieves and pressure. The framo was a booster hydraulic pump driven by a power take-off on the back of the main engine.

We caught two interesting by-catch species during the trip, one was a rarity, and the other was a curiosity.

The Ministry of Fisheries observer [Chris Petyt] eyes had lit up when he fished a Whalefish out of the cod end. His reference books were thumbed and he declared it the first New Zealand specimen of the Red Whalefish

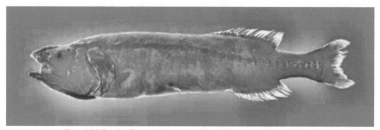

Red Whalefish 35 cm- [Te Papa collection]

Whalefish are named because they resemble whales [except they are a rib-less fish and many times smaller than the smallest whale]. The odd bit about Whalefish is the females are giants compared with the males and the males don't eat in adulthood.

Another trawl-shot had produced several cases of Bellows fish. The rough skinned Bellows fish have an iridescent silvery metallic appearance. Their unique features include a gritty sandpaper-surfaced drinking-straw snout and an awesome rear pointing multi-barbed spike.

Bellows fish 15cm- [T.Carter CSIRO]

Our Bellows fish were all the same size. 'Brylcream Barry' and I worked the port side. We collected a number of undamaged specimens and put them in the boiler vent space to dry them. When we got to port, he sold his for $5 each for 'piss money', which equated to $50 per kilo. I gave mine away to friends and acquaintances, and I guess they ultimately became dust catchers.

Surge - June [1994] ₒ ₒ ₒ ₒ

Surge reported the Conger-quota application was '*hiking along the paperwork trail*'. I hoped the paperwork was a long strider but it didn't worry me. In my mind, the Conger project had been downgraded [but not forgotten].

I was captivated by the Bellows fish, and I thought everybody should be too. I was over anxious to share.

"What are they worth as aquarium fish?" I asked people, who didn't care and weren't even a little interested. The question kept forcing its way out of my mouth and it became compulsive behaviour.

If I was given the slightness opportunity, I relayed details of their surface breaking leaps to friends and family.

"Their leaps make dolphins look pedestrian" and I raved about their colours *'so beautiful, they paled rainbows'*.

"They swim backwards, don't you know," I would say waving a dried Bellows fish under a victim's nose with a motion and tilt that showed off the iridescence to good effect.

"They can hover like a helicopter and swim straight up and down like the balls in a Galilean thermometer." I couldn't help myself and I would go on unsociably. "See these little fins just in front of the tail. They are like little stern thrusters. They can gyrate with a corrugation and it allows them to turn on an axis".

I was blinded by the moment, I raved on, and usually over-did it. I was like Tennysons *Ancient Mariner,* and once, I got close, [very close], to stopping a wedding party with a Bellows story. Such was the obsession and my need to share.

Grahame, in his wonderful *Treasury of New Zealand Fishes* said he had watched while they hovered and could only just discern movement in their fins.

It was easy to be captivated by the Bellows. I dreamed of a cost-effective way to catch them; and I dreamed of a worldwide operation dealing in live and dried Bellows fish but Surge didn't share the dream. He said he wouldn't catch fish that he couldn't eat.

***

The delays caused by the breakdowns, [delays you remember over a lifetime] combined with small catches and little reward, started scratching at the crews' insecurities. Doom and gloom was descending, despite the retainers being adequate.

Breakdowns were common at this stage. At sea there were regular periods when we were adrift with our *not under command* lights on. The vessel had sat idle in St Johns harbour New Foundland for a couple of years. Now it was being worked harder than ever before, in a much warmer climate, by fisherman and grounds which tested everything to breaking point.

Catches from the Challenger grounds had halved from the year before despite new fish areas being found. Doubts were creeping in, factions of thought were emerging, and the negative thinkers amongst us seemed to have the most persuasive voices.

Reg [AAOE] told the Lim family he would get the vessel working [paying its way] in six months. His 'no doubt' attitude assured some of us. By the end of June, we were broken down in Wellington after a second fruitless trip to the Challenger Plateau.

LOUISVILLE RIDGE
1995 - 2004 o o o o

3...The Louisville Ridge

Wellington Harbour - Aotea Quay [1995] ○ ○ ○ ○

While we were in port waiting for yet more vessel repairs to be completed, an unexpected event caused the New Zealand deep-sea trawling industry to change direction.

Photographs of sounder-displays showing large fish schools were being passed around the bridge by our management. The photographs had been taken on a leased vessel during survey work and they were exceptionally good. This was before digital cameras became 'the norm'. There was skill and trickery needed to take photos and get them back from the developer without the image being fragmented like a snap of a TV screen.

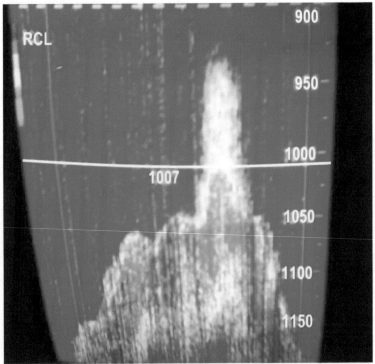

Sounder display : 80 metre fish mark above rock 1007 metres

Our company and the leased vessel had Chinese connections. The relationship brought the photos to our wheelhouse. The pictures were being handled with furtiveness and they caused much speculation. Riviera Rob said it was hard to read Asian body language, but [he hoped] what we were seeing was the deep and meaningful looks of greed.

The photos had the *Limmo gang*, [as we affectionately called the Lim family], running up our gangway. Some of us feared for their safety knowing the gangway was a dangerous passageway, sober or very sober [and especially at high tide].

The images started whispers which swept the decks from the officer's level down to the *pig pen* [where our *Billy Budds* had the bottom-most accommodation]. Some believed they depicted a new species of commercial fish and there were exotic names being bandied around.

The cook [Kung] was haunting the wheelhouse, offering chocolate éclairs and brandy snaps to maintain a presence. He reported to the mess the fish were a *deep-water Cod* and before an hour had passed, there was speculation about an antipodean cod war. Then rumours started about Russian gunboats on the way claiming a share of the fishery because of their Antarctic Territories.

Johnny [Winter], the Bosun, reckoned the Icelanders wouldn't be far behind. "They're obsessive when it comes to Cod." They wouldn't miss a Cod War; it doesn't matter where it is." He knew because he had worked with them on more than one occasion.

Whenever possible he squeezed in his favourite Icelandic story: "Do you know what the worst insult in Iceland is?" He asked the newest crewmembers and then after a pause, he answered the question himself, "Your mother's a crocodile!"

"That's fighting words in that part of the world," he said. He knew how to say it in Icelandic language as well.

"*Mamma pin Er crocadillia,*" he vocalized gutturally with a grotesque face – it was good acting. Most of us heard his Iceland stories too many times to be affected past a grin, but when Mahia Johnny found fresh ears it was still good amusement.

The fish names thrilled as each new rumour produced another fish: Patagonian Toothfish, Peruvian Oilfish, Steelnosed Bisonfish, Half-naked Hatchet Fish, and Magellan Plunderfish. Each had a moment or two of glory and the descriptions of what they looked like and the value of a full boatload were wondrous indeed.

The photographs had been taken at a position on the half-way line of the Louisville Ridge, seven hundred nautical miles past the Chatham Islands, in the Pacific Ocean.

The Ridge is an undersea structure stretching over a thousand nautical miles. Starting in the north at the juncture of the Tonga and Kermadec trenches at 30°s Latitude it goes down to a Fracture Zone at 48°s Latitude. None of the crew knew where the Louisville Ridge was, but it was agreed the name sounded like a fishing ground.

A search of the Wellington Library and National Library databases for the Louisville Ridge produced scant information. Most atlases and charts [including the large and impressive ones] did not include the Louisville Ridge. Its global space was used for title boxes or up-scaled inserts of the Pacific Islands.

All the official charts of the Louisville Ridge area [at the time] showed a partial outline of the undersea structure and some details of a feature called Valerie Guyot.

A Guyot is defined in the dictionary as a flat-topped submarine mountain pronounced "Ge`o" after Arnold Henri Guyot [1807 - 1884] a Swiss-born American geologist and geographer. Depth detail was non-existent and sounded depths rare, except for those at the Guyot.

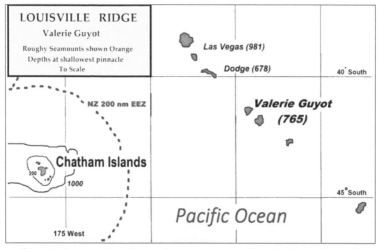

Chart : Louisville Ridge [showing position Valerie Guyot]

With the exception of the occasional long-line boat [following currents from the tropics] and Soviet expeditions [between 1982 and 1990], the Louisville Ridge had been fishing-boat free and was the last place to see any concentrated Roughy fishing in NZ`s corner of the planet.

Only a few species of fish live at the depths roughy fishers target and these fish have characteristics that are distinguishable from each other on a sounder display. The jury of 'photo evaluators' reached an opinion after a very long deliberation. It became official, the snaps showed Orange Roughy. Experts and sycophants agreed. It was the best news that year.

The photo verdict quickened pulses and enslaved electronic calculators. Factory figures [maximum days] were playing a part in the calculations of provisioning, profits, and dreams. At the time, putting a Louisville vessel to sea cost over a million dollars and rough weather [or breakdowns] could produce a trip with zero return. [Only speculators and gamblers need apply].

Bosun Ben ordered the net gear and as a result, we sailed with a full deck-store of spares [which made the trip a first and last time occasion].

When we arrived at the Ridge, we settled into a regular routine of mapping, harvesting and learning the new fish habits. Fishermen learn even small moves in distance can cause fish behaviour to change. Our fishing-masters had fished and learnt from the flats and hard edges of the New Zealand coast, but the Louisville Ridge had no coastal influence.

We had Swath charts and at the time, they were cutting-edge technology and a big advantage. They showed the likely fishing grounds at the Louisville Ridge. The charts had been produced using satellite imagery and highlighted the gravitational anomalies caused by the uplifting of the ocean surface where it passed over the Louisville Ridge. Swath charts were not to the scale of our sea charts but interpolation was easy using simple navigation instruments.

We used *search and rescue pattern* [creeping line of advance] to map the submarine structures at target-depth advancing a sounder beam width apart [one tenth of a nautical mile]. The prime target-depth for Orange Roughy is between 700 and 1100 metres, although off New Zealand bags of fish have been caught from 450 metres and down to 1300 metres.

When the boundaries of the under-ocean structure had been established, the gaps would be filled in by steering at right angles to the edges and escarpments to produce a sounder picture. The most accurate depths and the right-angle courses lessened side-lobe distortion and graphically produced an exact contour on the plotter.

Side lobe is a fuzzy effect caused by the return-signals being reflected from the craggy rock faces and at times, they can look like a school of fish. Areas which produce side-lobe echoes are also a good habitat for schools of Roughy because the side-lobe confuses their predators' [whales] echolocation. The opposite applies. If the plot soundings eliminate the side-lobe and later side-lobe appears, then the signal is fish. Modern sounders have memory which is useful tool for double-checking.

A big school of fish will mask the rock they are schooled above or the seabed. Thorough plotting, records the exact rock structure and when it is under a school of fish, the clearances are certain. This information can save a lot of net mending. A minor rip-up can take over six hours to mend.

There were thousands of square miles to plot at the Louisville Ridge and plotting is best done at slow speed of around four knots [walking speed]. The slow speed ensures an accurate plot and shows any fish-marks clearly. The slowness can be tiresome for some, but it is high adrenalin time for a keen roughy fisherman seeking a discovery.

It was staggering the number of times hurriedly mapped areas produced fish when they were searched thoroughly. There was always the chance you would stumble over a school but the best results came from crossing and re-crossing of the grounds. Thorough mapping was a major reason for our success.

A trip off - [Memories of my father] ₀ ₀ ₀ ₀

I had my first time off after a year at sea. There should have been more breaks, but the crew rotation system had failed from the start. I had worked over ten months at sea with only a few short port calls ashore.

My time off was a time of reflection. My birth father [Roy] had died while I was at sea and I missed his funeral. Long fishing trips can cause you to miss funerals, birthdays, and family reunions.

Before we sailed I rang my father to say, "See you after the next trip". He replied prophetically "You better hurry up; I'm closer to the post than most."

It was his way of talking, yet somehow I thought he would live forever [or at least close to it]. I went to his homeland at Wild Cattle Hill, Port Levy and gathered rock [andesite] to mark his North Island resting place. My memories of him were his simple lessons, his gifted way with animals and his sayings:

`Thistles are only a sign of a healthy paddock`
`Best way to climb a hill is straight at it`.
...and he had a shepherds' lament,
`You can walk through a paddock on a dark night, and all you can hear, is the horses eating.`

He worked high-country farms most of his life. His loathing of foot-rot dictated it and he could talk [in the rain] about Coopworths....sometimes it seemed the only thing we had in common was a love of cheese-and-raw-onion sandwiches.

***

My return to the boat was memorable. Riviera Rob had bailed me up before I got out of the car. He was in a mood - the vigour of his chuddy-gum chewing telegraphed it.

"What a hoot - you know how the bludgers have been pinching my smokes?" he asked, looking for recognition but not an answer. He was itching to tell the story. One thing about Riviera, when he had a good tale [or a bit of gossip], he shared it. He started talking excitedly. The chatter was somewhat confiding [and bonding], but not his normal behaviour.

"I got them, I got them," he howled, repeating it with glee. I guessed he was talking about the young crew who regularly stole the tailor-made smokes from his cabin. He had taken an anger management course about his smokes and the deckhands.

I asked him how? It was an obligatory question; I was thinking a surveillance camera or fingerprint dust.

"Best I ever thought of, bloody creatures of habit, I let them think they were getting away with it and every bloody day they would empty the part-packet of smokes I left on my dresser."

His chuddy mastication reached fever pitch and his eyes went wild. He looked like he'd just won a big prize [in some places, his behaviour would have been described as a conniptions].

"Then this morning while the whole crew were in the mess having breakfast, I went in there." He was having little waves of laughter. "I got their attention, and told them there wouldn't be any ciggies in my cabin tomorrow."

"I said, if you have been taking them, you better know, for the last week every smoke I left there has been stuck up my bum the length of the filter and gently rotated both clockwise and anti-clockwise."

He looked at me, his moustache lopsided by a curl in his upper lip. He started a grin, best described as wicked and probably the same as the grin he was wearing, when he told them.

"It was instantaneous," his voice was loud, his chin went up and his nose pierced the air, he was pumped. "One of them regurgitated a coloured mixture of half-digested cereals with fruity-yogurt bindings and another bastard needed a back-bashing after swallowing his coffee the wrong way. Love it - don't you love it?'" His toes tapped the wharf and he started to repeat the story, but this time, naming the culprits and adding the bits he had left out or forgotten in the first telling.

Riviera Rob had revenge on a crew who had never given him much respect. Thieving was never a problem on this boat, but I suppose the crew thought an unpopular Bosun [with tailor-made smokes] was fair game. Riviera Rob revelled in his unpopularity because it made it easy for him to give the hard orders.

January – [1996] ○ ○ ○ ○

After two years of fishing the Louisville Ridge, our weekly retainers had dropped from $1000 to $500 a week. We were averaging two hundred tonnes of product worth $1.6m per trip. With our catch percentages [the crew's share was divided out of 25% of the catch value] earnings averaged $800 /week.

The vessel was working well as most parts of the boat had been modified to improve production. By this stage the factory coped with close to thirty tonnes of product a day [up from seventeen]. Luck rarely showed its hand. Generally it was long hours of close observations, careful appraisal of trawls and much net mending. But the luckiest incident happened to Stinky [Bryant] after he set up a pinnacle trawl on a good mark, west side [290 degrees] just off its 918-metre top.

Perhaps it was a distraction or maybe false instrument read-outs but he hit the seamount at 1060 metres [142 metres below its summit] and was immediately fast, wrapped around the seamount like a kite on a power line. The gear came off the seamount quickly, and before his red face had time to shine, the result was a fifty tonne catch. Captain Cunliffe yelled "Las Vegas!" and from then on another seamount got its fishing name. It was new fishing country and seamounts were being named on a daily basis. Some names have stuck to this day and other names are still creating argument.

Not far from *Las Vegas* is a seamount called *Dodge*. It was the starting point for our first traverse survey of the Louisville Ridge. We found a large school of fish on a knob [in the *Pins* group] but it took time to work out a tow angle and a landing depth. The situation was slowed because the fish were only showing once a day around the midnight hours.

On our third night, we were in position waiting for the fish to school up. The trawl shot was set up. Silence reigned in the wheelhouse with all eyes on the trawl electronics, but no one was on radar watch. Every bit of collective concentration was aimed at capturing the fish. We were about to turn and shoot the net down the stern-ramp when a deckhand reported he could see a vessel's lights *"looms and twinkles* on the edge of the horizon."

There was a good chance we had been sprung on the spot which is like a home invasion in the solitude of ocean fishing.

Our radars located the voyeur at seven sea miles and observation of its lights suggested it was Russian built[1]. We started doing deceptive tricks to keep the other trawler guessing.

We did dummy tows and false run-backs over some very nasty ground and deep abysmal-plains hoping to confuse the interloper. We acted like a busy boat mimicking a catch coming on-board, but they kept a position seven miles distant.

The intruder was on radio silence. We suspected there might be Kiwis on board and it was a leased vessel from a Soviet trawler fleet based in Lyttelton. Expensive satellite phone calls didn't clarify the mystery. You couldn't help wondering if they knew about the fish already or whether they were a scout vessel sent to find us. Our radar plotting revealed they weren't fishing or searching for fish.

Every time we moved away from the seamount, the stalking vessel stayed equidistant. They would be reporting our position to their management and someone would be selling the information to other fishing companies. We tried sneaking up on them but they shied away. It was obvious they were determined to stay and spy.

---

[1] Russian boats have bright white light and Asian vessels have a teal gas colour.

On the second night of the 'cat-and-mouse manoeuvres' we named the seamount *Dodge,* although it wasn't clear which vessel was the most artful dodger. We were on full radio-watch and it was heartening we didn't hear any Kiwi voices on the radiophone channels.

The Russian fleet [without exception] return good radar signals because of their high flat sides. The major difference between them and us was the radars. We had three radars in our wheelhouse. Two had come with the boat from Canada; they were tuned for icebergs, and very good for close and medium distance detection. Before the Louisville operations began, our AAOE had fitted the latest high-end-model radar. The *war toy* had its scanner high on our mast. It showed target echoes out to twenty-five miles and it could plot other fishing boats over the horizon.

After three days of fucking-around and raising our frustration levels, our AAOE relieved the situation. "They can't find their own fish and I won't give them 'our' fish," he said and we started steaming south at full speed.

The Swath charts showed over a dozen indications of *high country* and we used courses that didn't divulge our intentions. After thirty-six hours, we doubled back with our lights out and the wheelhouse watch doubled. Our radars were tuned for maximum coverage and the radio direction finder was ready. When we were sure the other vessel was not following we continued south on a voyage of discovery.

The southern passage took five days and stretched as far as the *Lynx's* insurance cover allowed. We couldn't help but think about all the fish we'd left behind and the resoluteness of the AAOE's decision to leave them there.

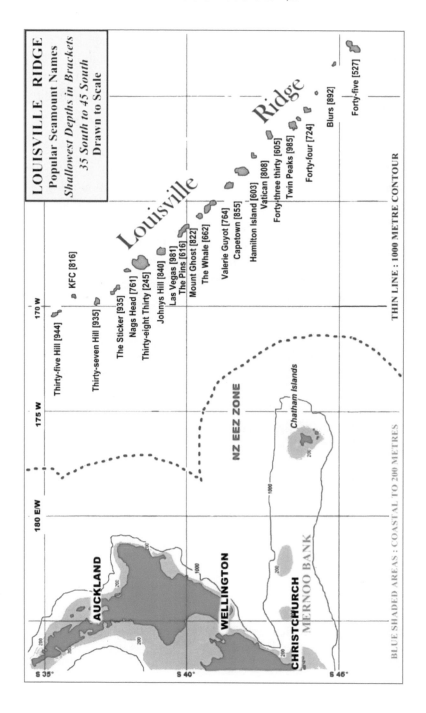

LOUISVILLE RIDGE
Popular Seamount Names
Shallowest Depths in Brackets
35 South to 45 South
Drawn to Scale

Louisville

Ridge

Thirty-five Hill [944]
KFC [816]
Thirty-seven Hill [935]
The Sticker [935]
Nags Head [761]
Thirty-eight Thirty [245]
Johnys Hill [840]
Las Vegas [981]
The Pins [616]
Mount Ghost [822]
The Whale [662]
Valerie Guyot [764]
Capetown [855]
Hamilton Island [603]
Vatican [808]
Forty-three thirty [605]
Twin Peaks [985]
Forty-four [724]
Blurs [892]
Forty-five [527]

NZ EEZ ZONE

Chatham Islands

MERNOO BANK

AUCKLAND

WELLINGTON

CHRISTCHURCH

THIN LINE : 1000 METRE CONTOUR

BLUE SHADED AREAS : COASTAL TO 200 METRES

170 W
175 W
180 E/W

S 35°
S 40°
S 45°

Recording lines of soundings and making plots kept everyone busy while we traversed north again. Dale [fishing mate] named most of the new seamounts with panache and genius. Future expeditions proved we only missed three fishing grounds.

Twenty-one days later, we arrived back at the *Dodge knob* with twenty tonnes of product in the hold and a good plot of the lower Louisville Ridge. The plot became the foundation of future fishing expeditions and the search for new spawn areas.

We approached the Dodge knob with apprehension and circled it wide doing Radar sweeps to make sure it was clear. Twenty-four hours of reconnoitre proved the Russian vessel had gone and the fish were still there!

The first bag of fish was a big one and we were a tender vessel. It was a 'witch-doctor' special and probably demonstrated his patience had evaporated. Big first-bags are avoided because they are dangerous [for stability]. A hundred tonnes of fish on deck with little in the holds or fuel tanks can tip a boat over. Our first bag listed the boat and tested Ivan's [chief engineer] ballasting skills. Ballasted it was a list, the boat could resist.

The AAOE [as was normal] bellowed over the ships speakers "Cut the beckets[1], cut the beckets, cut the beckets…"

He repeated it until the last becket was cut. With the beckets cut, the bag's centre of gravity was lowered and the catch became less likely to roll towards the low side of our unstable vessel.

---

[1] Beckets are the lateral reinforcement around the cod end, they restrict the cod-end from swelling out bigger than the width of the stern- ramp and are handy strops for tipping the cod end into the fish pound.[see Notated photo chapter 10.]

The risky first bag started a steady processing cycle which continued until we had over two hundred tonnes of product in the hold. We were forced to finish fishing and return to port because of low fuel, a lack of packaging and a shortage of food.

The trip had been a lesson in both patience and ballasting.

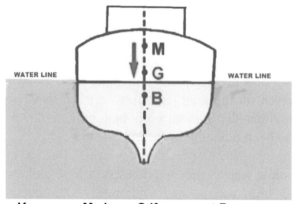

Keep your M above G if you want Buoyancy

4...Rip-ups...Fill-ups & Dire Warnings

Napier - February [1996] ₒ ₒ ₒ ₒ

There had been changes. Our base had moved to Port Napier because a local meat works had closed and there was low cost cool storage available. We were unloading after Christmas at sea and two new crewmen had joined the boat. You could have been forgiven for thinking [aloud], *where did they come from?* It was obvious the rumour mill had broken down and the AAOE had been planning in secret.

The new crew were Asian and dressed in Mao jackets, pyjama pants and blue canvas caps. Strange sights occur on big trawlers, but the strangest ones always seem to happen at the wharf. The new crew were part of a fishing company which had dealings with our management. One was a stout captain and the other was his slim attendant and interpreter. They shared a cabin on the deckhands' level and they ate in their cabin, sitting side by side on the bottom bunk. They ate with the cabin door open to the passageway and when we passed and looked inside, they smiled and indicated by clicking chop sticks at their lips, that they thought the food was good.

The captain would work as a deckhand while his interpreter would work in the factory, but both would be on shift at the same time for communications. It was a good arrangement and it allowed the captain to see how our boat operated, for future fishing ventures.

44

When the captain was on deck with us he had no interpreter but he was quick on the pickup. "smoko", "munchies" and "many sluts gooda" quickly became part of his vernacular. Deckhand [Ruds] taught him how to talk like an east coaster.

He became known as Captain Munchies and the name lit up his face when it was used. Munchies became his favourite word. He would say *'munchies',* anticipating smoko and - when sea-eggs were trawled and landed intact.

He could be a bit greedy about the sea-eggs and would track an egg-filled cod-end up the deck, following it so determinedly that he could have pushed rugby packs aside. He was never beaten to a sea-egg while he was on the Lynx.

Munchies slurped his sea-eggs, devouring them with a little tomalley dribble. He only stopped slurping to smile. When he finished feasting, he had the look of an oyster lover [at the start of the season]. Some of his taste buds and genes were incredible attracted to those urchins.

"He starts a mend with a larks-head on the bar" noted Riviera Rob, who'd had his big nose in his knot book [again].

"Just shows there's more than one way to fuck up a net mend," bantered back decky Davey Jack, who stuck with sheet-bends.

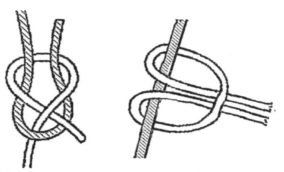

Sheet bend [or Weavers knot]   Larks head [or Cow hitch]

Captain Munchies knew the words *bodge* and *bodgey* [no interpreter needed]. He understood the root meaning of the word and the degree of acceptable *bodgeying*. Nets were getting 'bodgey jobs' because of damage done at the new grounds, and Munchies bodgeyed them his way. There was a lot of mending going on and it was *'bag of fish or belly-out'* times and sometimes both.

Captain Munchies was from Dalian [where the Yangtze meets the Yellow Sea], and in the normal course of action was the captain of the Geng Hai, a large factory trawler [previous Wesermunde: built 1973 at Bremerhaven]. The Geng Hai had been to the Louisville Ridge in 1994 and this played a big part in our fishing direction.

Captain Munchies was hard working and before long it didn't seem strange a captain of such a big boat was working on our deck. In turn, Munchies learnt [at sea level] how big the sea had to be to stop our fishing operations. Our captains would only stop fishing when *tested* wires and chains started breaking. Wild-sea trawling was their specialty.

The Geng Hai [3577 GT] Shooting the gear at The Ridge.

At the end of the season, Reg [AAOE], Riviera Rob, and Ruds went to the Geng Hai with Captain Munchies. They would search the Pacific Ocean and return to fill up [holds and domestic freezers] at the Louisville Ridge. This was the biggest load caught at the Louisville Ridge.

I went back to school to study for a deep-sea maritime ticket, a qualification which took twelve weeks of study.

Whenever you return to a vessel after a break, there are always changes and on this occasion, there had been crew changes.

The trawl and factory decks had become infiltrated with East Coasters. The coasters came on-board [in ones], and brought with them a new language. When their numbers grew, *boil-ups* became regular meals [whether the cooks liked it or not].

Louisville Ridge - [1996] ₒ ₒ ₒ ₒ

The third off-season catches [October to May] were dropped and only three boats were working the Ridge year-round. When we had first arrived at the Louisville it hadn't mattered it was off-season. It had been almost effortless to locate Roughy. Finding a safe tow was the time consuming part of the fishing operations.

In the early years a sixty-tonne catch, was a good bag. At times, these resident schools were large but two years down the track, the schools had become bifurcated and in some places more than once. The baitfish had gained an advantage and when their numbers grew, they would spill out to the Roughy secondary feeding areas and start a new cycle. The smaller schools were harder to track down and the task needed the patience of an inshore trawler-man. Good catches were still to be had, but not as often. Twenty-five tonnes was a good bag.

Two years of fishing had seen whale numbers drop off. When we had first explored the middle seamounts of the Ridge, there had been a resident group with several outriders *on-station*. Exploration found there were two groups along the Ridge, but two years later, the whale pods had fewer outriders.

Whale numbers had been reduced and so had the fishing vessels fishing the ridge and the overall fleet had been reduced by two-thirds.

47

1996 was a terrific Roughy spawn-season with a couple of good loads and a *'fill-up'* finish.

The AAOE had come back to our vessel when the Geng Hais` exhaust started showing thick black-smoke of the engine surrender. His arrival was timely [suspiciously so] because we had just found the main spawn mark. While the Geng Hai left a smoke-trail all the way to the horizon, we eagerly showed the AAOE our fish mark on the sounder memory. He lied [like any ordinary fisherman] saying, "I had a mark that was bigger."

We had ARPA and we had been plotting his every movement. He hadn`t been anywhere near a fish mark. His lie was part of what made him the AAOE and in line with his tenet of *'never let anyone know what you don't know.'*

He complained about the coffee and the sounder settings and bumped up the gain from 4 to 7. We had been using his gain settings since he left the boat a year and half before, in fact we had used all his settings,. The cycles, the pulse repetition rate, and the Hosie number were his.

The AAOE settings had been sacrosanct. They had been computer memorized, printed, and placed in safe places, and because of their perceived value, copies had been purloined. He bumped the gain from 4 to 7 without a second thought.

The AAOE began a sequence of catches which put our factory-line into maximum production. He kept the catches coming on-board until we were out of freezer space. It had taken three spawn seasons to get our first *fill-up*.

It was a time for reflection and evaluation. The AAOE had shown us how to fill a trawler, but there was no doubt it was a once in a lifetime catch for the boat. I'd lost twenty thousand dollars on expectations, but I felt as if I was part of the big catch and that felt good.

***

Dire Warnings o o o o

August 1996 New Zealand Fisheries Minister D.Kidd was spreading the Louisville Ridge news. He went public:

> *'But roughly 100 miles beyond our zone is the Louisville Ridge along which rich orange roughy grounds were discovered a few years ago. Biologically we cannot claim these are straddling stocks. So we have no jurisdiction. The Law of the Sea Convention gives no teeth to us as the nearest coastal state, or to any other. So we have seen vessels from several nations, as well as Australians and New Zealanders, rape and pillage these stocks. Our fishers say they cannot afford to let the chance go by and let others carry it all away. That it understandable, even though it is wrong in principle, but principle has nothing to do with the high seas yet. What is the result so far? Naturally there is no reliable data on captures but my private gleanings at home and abroad indicate that catches are down to a third of those only three years ago and the fishery is expected to be abandoned within a couple of years'.*

The bit about *'abandonment in a couple of years'* had us thinking. It seemed like we had only started, and there were countless seamounts and gullies still to search. Fisheries only get abandoned because of economics, not because the stocks have disappeared and we knew the stocks were still high. Kidd was making an early call.

Wellington - October [1996] o o o o

There had been changes while I'd been away fishing – the Post Office had been abandoned. It was gone, from a windswept Willis Street location to an even windier alleyway at Marion Square. The new PO had a chorus of deep-voiced and no doubt, deep-throated transvestites offering non-postal services at its entrance [after hours].

49

The breezy Wellington wharf side was a rattle of ropes on steel. The wind had a bite to it as I walked back from town, after emptying my post office box of its contents. There was a full load of mail, a common result of being two months at sea. Horizontal southerly rain was stinging my eyes by the time I got to our gangplank.

In the warmth of my cabin, the first envelope I opened was from the Queensland Fish Management Authority offering free certificated training courses. I had qualified as a master fisherman some years earlier and kept up the membership. You could smell sunshine on the envelope and the flyer said boldly...

TRAIN THE TRAINERS - ASSESS THE ASSESSORS

The courses were part of *Hazard Analysis and Critical Control,* a quality system that was a space industry spin off. Master Fisherman in Queensland would need to do these courses to manage product and prepare it for export to the European Union. European export licenses required trained and assessed crew somewhere in the early part of the products process chain.

The mail made my mind wandered a little further north, to the tropics. It flittered away, you could say. I sent my resignation by telex using the vessels communications system, [there and then] and felt good about it.

I began to pack up my cabin of eighteen months. It was a confrontation with the evidence of retail-therapy clothes [worn once] and work clothes [worn out]. I had only had two breaks during the three years I'd spent on the boat and both time-outs had been busy.

'Don't look back', is a common phrase about leaving a boat, but I did. I couldn't resist the impulse. The Lynx had been my first ship and it had been good to me. When I looked back, I saw the anchor [over a tonne of it], hanging loose from its hawse pipe and I was immediately reminded of many sleepless nights from its banging on the hull. My next boat, I thought, would have an anchor that didn't crash the hull like a pile driver.

Surge - October [1996] ₒ ₒ ₒ ₒ

I told Surge, I was going to Queensland and he reported the Conger project had stalled. *'Every species will be introduced into the quota system, you'll just have to wait'* was the official line. Surge reported, tongue in cheek, the Conger incarcerators [there were now three of them] were handling it well and he went on about the new trap designs he was working on.

After Hutton [Treasury of New Zealand Fishes]

"It's take your pick for me, Surge," I interrupted him, "They're doing courses all along the coast and I thought I might do one in Cairns and the other in Rockhampton a month later. I'll visit the harbours, towns, and friends on the trip between."

"Some people have all the luck," Surge said. Then he turned my mind in a spin by adding, "I think Sue and I are breaking up. My bet is she leaves before Xmas."

"I've been thinking, she'll make a good ex-wife." He added and before going silent.

It was sad, only for the union. They were both lovely people. It was just Surge's ambition to 'tinker to retirement' that didn't match Sue's ambition, or even come close to it.

Surge liked to plan and procrastinate. He could easily turn a short-term plan into a lifetime goal, and most of his plans had the sniff of salt air about them. Sue didn't like the ocean. She likened success to middle class comfort and that was hard to find on the Pakahi with a landlocked salt-water fisherman.

§

5...МNTAHИE & MUTINY

Wellington - May [1997] ○ ○ ○ ○

Lambton Harbour was busy when I went looking for a job. On the wharf crew, technicians and providores were working hard to get boats ready for a new Roughy season.

I was back from Australia and keen to go fishing but there were no vacancies. I was ready to accept anything offered - *'any boat, any job, or any fishery'*. A wardrobe of tropical clothes and jandals in Wellingtons wintry May weather can do that to you.

Wellington - June [1997] ○ ○ ○ ○

June arrived, the Roughy boats starting heading out to the grounds and I still had no job or prospects. I was at the sharp end of acute anxiety and contemplating a new career.

The perturbation passed when a local fishing company I had been pestering for a position, gave me the phone number of a Singaporean vessel owner [Michael]. I rang Michael, who was in Auckland. His accent was Asian with an occasional pronunciation suggesting a private-school education [there was a hint of toffee on the nose] and hastily I agreed to meet at his motel.

The 800-kilometre trip north to the meeting passed quickly. My mind was busy working out all the considerations for the work contract and everything needed to get the vessel ready for the fishing trip. This was definitely the biggest undertaking I had tackled in my life. The vessel was 55 metres long and I was in charge.

Michael was staying at a brightly lit Parnell motel, but in a poorly lit part of the complex and it looked like the staff-accommodation. The building was a large, once grand, three-storeyed house, with ornate gabled barges and small bay windows. The cobweb-covered bay windows had flower boxes with blistered paint and dishevelled shingled shelter-roofs. The heavy cobwebs where white with age and layered with kill carcasses.

Time had taught me you were likely to meet fishing-vessel owners in strange places. The house was sign-posted *Chalets 1-4* and inside was a large dark hallway. A fire-alarm call box, shining brightly [like a port navigation-light] was the only lighting.

Michael answered Chalet 2`s door. Inside the living room, the only furniture was a small kitchen table with a tired formica top. The carpet was threadbare and the seating was backless stools with peeling chromed legs.

The lounge looked like it had been furnished from an Op Shop [at sale time]. In my time I`d seen homeless drunks living under bridges who had more furniture and it was obvious that largesse wasn't going to be part of the contract.

Introductions and brief histories were exchanged – we learnt we had both trained as quantity surveyors. We discussed how close the job had taken us to death by boredom. It also meant we could chuckle about 'united inches', 'foot board measures', 'British thermal units' and 'bunce' during awkward moments of conversation.

He excused his surroundings saying his ex-partners had lived in the motels proper for a couple of years, but he preferred to save money by staying in the chalets, adding they were, "Unfurnished but just as close to the wharves."

Michael had come to New Zealand with a group of gold mining speculators from Kalgoorlie [Australia] when Roughy catches had boomed in 1993. Michael stayed on when the others departed for other parts of the globe to continue their high-living speculative lifestyle. He had an easy smile and a pleasant manner but I couldn't help thinking he probably had bullet scars [armpit to armpit] under his shirt.

The season had already begun at the Louisville Ridge and we were both desperate to get there, so our discussions were completed with haste and a handshake. The agreement was that Michael would employ a captain to ensure the vessel was manned to comply with the regulations, and the fishing was left to me. My share of the catch was four and half per cent of sales and he agreed to equip the vessel to my satisfaction.

The Komtek II [Miss Greeny] GT 1390 LOA 59m

The next day we met at Wynyard Wharf. The fishing vessel *Komtek II* was a high-sided Russian trawler and it had a centre gantry as a distinguishing feature.

Michael called the boat *Miss Greeny*. The hull was freshly painted green [his lucky colour] and it was a reminder of the superstitions vessel owners bring to the industry. It would be interesting to know how much green is needed for a fishing-boat to be lucky. The rest of the vessel was brown with rust [and neglected rust at that]. I couldn't help thinking it might have been luckier if both sides and not just the wharf side of the hull had been painted green.

It was obvious the vessel was minimally maintained but some encouragement could be taken from the fact the Russian crew hadn't jumped ship. The fish factory had weeping pipes, dripping taps and controls featuring temporary repairs. Sheets of plastic had been hung from high places to divert the leaks from the processing areas.

The maritime survey authorities had deemed *Komtek* seaworthy, so this resolved some of the doubts in my mind. We placed orders for pipe-fixing material and our *Wrap-It* pipe-bandage order probably cornered the NZ market.

Bosun Dan and factory manager Jerzy had worked the boat since its arrival in NZ. The cook was a new cook because the previous one had been a wife-murderer-in-hiding who had been arrested without fuss when the vessel docked.

The Russian captain however had been recruited from the New Zealand unemployment register. Our biggest problem was we didn't have any crew [deck or factory hands]. We tried the deep-sea crew register, but it was no help. We advertised in the New Zealand Herald for crew, the ad attracted the keen men [and layabouts] of Auckland and they were late for interviews.

The first seven people who knew what a Yo-Yo or Lancaster was, were employed as deckhands. The others, if they could name a fishing boat they had worked, were sent down to the factory manager.

The new crew was a true measure of what you'd expect at a late stage of the season. They had minimal experience and lots of dreams [including the Russian Captain and me]. They assured us they had worked on fishing boats of one type or other, but their sea stories seemed bloated. Nautical nervousness was everywhere and their conversations provided dreadful eavesdropping.

My own nervousness wasn't helped after a deck visit, when I had watched a deckhand securing a fish-case full of bobbin washers. He tied the case up with a dozen or more granny knots. In some places, they would have called the rope-work, 'end to end bends'. The decky secured his job when he told me he'd done Blue Cod fishing off Stewart Island with Jimmy [Aorere] and because of this I'd showed him favouritism.

With no regard for the consequences, I asked "Where did you learn to tie those knots?"

He looked me in the eye and with prideful manner answered "On the farm!" His voice had a soft Southland burr, his naiveté bloomed, and it pacified my anger moment. "Probably just three will do, because you never know when you'll have to undo things in a hurry – and don't lose your knife." I wished I hadn't added the last bit as it created nervous looks.

The selected crew [there were rejections] except for the two bosuns, had no deep-sea experience, and we proposed to do a ten-week trip to the Louisville Ridge. It wasn't exactly a dream set up.

The Russian Captain was tall and over groomed. He revealed himself as an ex-submariner with only two fishing trips experience. Those trips were Hoki trawling off the West Coast, which was far removed from our undertaking. The Russian crew rumoured he was an ex-commissar, but this didn't mean much to the Kiwi crew. He spoke good English and he had a love of the classics [written and musical]. His nautical knowledge was sound and he was easily led into arguments on political ideology. He was fond of saying, "If I am wrong, I will shoot myself and you will not need a firing squad."

My wandering thoughts wondered if submarine commissar was promotion up or demotion down from salt mine commissar. Ship's safety was his responsibility and the fishing was mine. He would not take orders from a *'fishing master'* and insisted I was to be called the *Commander* [in the navy this is a rank below Captain]. The rank flattered and embarrassed me.

It took a few days to ready things and just before we sailed, the Maritime Safety Authority requested we run both fire and abandon ship drills in their presence. It was a reasonable request considering the lack of experience on board the vessel.

We sailed after the drill and sat at anchor until a bit after midnight to avoid a Friday the thirteenth departure. Fridays are a superstitiously bad day to set sail on a fishing trip. The significance of this bad omen was not lost on anyone and our Singaporean owner, Michael, said he would light some incense at the Sea Dragon Temple when he returned to the East.

That night we left the Rangitoto Roads, a few minutes after midnight. We sounded the ship's horn to awake the *Sea Dragon* and let Michael in his dingy chalet know we were underway. He rang us with his best wishes and said he'd heard the horn blasts.

Louisville Ridge - [1997] ○ ○ ○ ○

Our plan was to go to the Seamount at 35°south. The seamount is the closest to NZ and its spawn spot had been elusive. The 35°s seamount is sited at a transition point of the Louisville Ridge and is more influenced by the gyres of the Kermadec Ridge than the push of the Southern Ocean

The seamount had been named *Last Chance* when we first visited it, because it was the last seamount to be mapped. It was odd the closest seamount to any New Zealand port had been the last one to be explored. When the Ridge was first fished, the Roughy spawn times and the latitudes governed fishing area decisions, so proximity was not a factor.

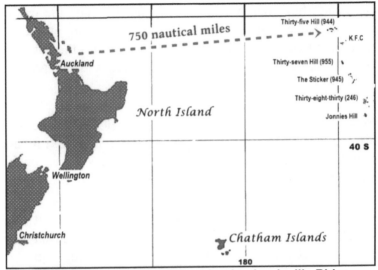

KOMTEK II course from Auckland to Louisville Ridge

We would use the seamount to test gear and I had a gambler's belief I could find the undiscovered spawn aggregation. The travelling time out to *Chance* was used to assemble the fishing gear and ready the factory.

I planned to read the ship's manuals and get familiar with the bridge controls. '*Read your manuals*' had been a repeated phrase during my periods of nautical training.

The manuals were in Russian and neither the English speaking Russian captain nor the expensive Oxford translation dictionaries were helpful in unravelling the non-default operating instructions. Technical words involving electronics don't translate easily.

At night, it was impossible to see the instruments because there seemed no way to turn on the wheelhouse lights. If I asked where the light switch was, I got blank looks. It was obvious that there was a concerted conspiracy to keep me in the dark.

Normally wheelhouse lights are above the helm or fishing station and they are red to minimize glare and reflection. The light fittings were on the ceiling and I replaced the bulbs, but they didn't light up. The wheelhouse lights were dead and the only lighting was the twenty-four volt emergency lights but they were only as bright as a candle.

I had middle-aged eyesight failure and under-strength glasses. I started to worry the dimness would make the fishing operation a difficult start up. The pitch control and the autopilot looked like they had been part of a fifties sputnik system. The components were stark with no LED readouts or backlighting. There had to be a wheelhouse light switch somewhere, it was a certainty. There was a circuit breaker in the fuse box, it was the only one labelled in English, and it suggested a well-worn path.

The more I looked for the light switch, the more frantic I became. My brain was starting to fall out of gear and move into loose-sprocket neutral. It was my first trip as a solo fisherman. I envisaged all the problems I might encounter but I hadn't thought a small worry, like a light switch, would undermine my confidence.

The wheelhouse walls were covered in gadgetry. One wall had a boxed electric-pulse swing-arm instrument recording the vessel's course. The machine spewed out a wide ribbon of paper, but there wasn't a switch behind the paper curtain. Close to the track recorder was a Geiger-counter, a relic from the cold war. All Soviet trawlers of the time had them. [I treated boredom just looking and thinking about the Geiger.]

Next to the radiation counter was a phone apparatus that looked like a giant snail shell. It was a handset made for communications in a nuclear holocaust, when a radiation blast might sear your lips to your ears. There were distractions aplenty but no light switch.

I replaced random searching with a systematic approach from the ceiling-bulkhead down. It took time. Switching and button bashing [to the max] only proved an alien logic had been put to work at the design stage.

59

"Let there be light" I started saying in soft tones with childlike rhyme and repetition. My search went on determinedly. Every knob and switch from head height to Soviet naval belly-button level was tweaked.

Eureka! In a small recess, in a place not too different from where European car-manufacturers hide a bonnet release, I found a small button with serrated edges. The un-grouted label had the engraved capital letters МNТАНИЕ.

The button had a twiddle knob. It was the wheelhouse light switch incorporating a dimmer-control. Perhaps it was hidden away for safety because it was positioned where only the helmsman could use it. Things got easier, I had been feeling the pressure of the task ahead and the thoughts of having to do it in the dark hadn't helped.

The ships plotters had been wiped clean of their fishing information. I only had one disc and it was very basic. It wasn't an ideal situation, but I did have a relief map of the Louisville Ridge in my memory and I knew parts of it as one knows their own neighbourhood.

You have to be lucky if you want to be a fisherman and luck was on our side. The manual reading produced the fishing information we needed. Fortunately, we found it before we got to the grounds. In a bookshelf which held seldom-used nautical publications, the type helpful if you are seeking the light characteristics of a beacon off Malagassi [or the height of the Tallahassee Bridge], was a book which changed the trip.

Most manuals on the shelf were written in Cyrillic cryptic but amongst them was a handwritten diary, in English, with copybook-style lettering and skilful contrasting penmanship. Luck had moved our way because it was Sekopes records.

Sekope was the Komtek's previous skipper and a veteran of the Nelson Roughy fishing fleet. He was a renowned Roughy fisherman from Tonga and a product of the New Zealand/Pacific Islands training scheme.

He had completed twelve trips as skipper on the *Komtek*, starting in September 1994. I checked the big numbers first - *Total Catch 850 tonnes of product.*

His peak catch had been 265 tonnes of product on a trip during the spawn of 1995 [June]. His worst trip was Trip 10 starting in March 96. It recorded a 'no catch' result, a lost door, and main engine failure.

The diary was a full record of the trawls for all the Komteks' trips. It contained details of everything: wind, sea, barometer readings, and global positions [start and finish] for every trawl. It had the depths landed and picked up and the catch landed. It took time to read but I likened the book to a hunting story. There were 1364 entries. I transferred the trawl shots, one by one, trip by trip, into the ships plotter using colour coding. Entering the tows in the plotter was like going fishing with Sekope [graphically].

The entries showed areas of concentrated fishing effort for the major seamounts and it became apparent the fishing log covered most of the grounds. Our information pool had become as good as the rest of the fleet. Working out a tow can sometimes take hours and cause doubt and headaches, but we had been gifted them in copybook handwriting.

Two days later, we had our first trawl-shot. We shot the trawl on a safe tow without looking for fish marks *'shot it blind'*, as they say. The catch was a half-tonne of Roughy with roes that were stage 3, which is a ripe roe about a month before the spawn proper.

The result was a conversation changer and a buzz went around vessel. One young Russian was bubble buoyant with the sight of the Roughy.

"It is a good sight that orange, not for one year have I seen it so orange beautiful," he said with smiles and bad English. His comment was more than encouraging.

I hadn't seen the young Russian during the trip out to grounds. He was the sort you didn't mind hanging around the wheelhouse and his absence had been noticeable. When I asked the Kiwi Bosun about it he told me the young Russians had been in their cabins with 'caverjects[1] and centrefolds'. The answer pricked my prudery and took my mind off fishing for more than a moment.

We found a small fish mark to trawl. The mark produced half-tonne bags of fish and two tonne of product for the day. Our hopes were high. The gear had performed well and we didn't need many `new season` fish to feel good. I was learning on the run and had to work at hiding my inexperience with the fast-speed electric winches [rather than the hydraulic ones I was used to].

The next morning at the change of light, our trawl-tow was a '*fast`ner*' and we were left anchored to the bottom. Tide and wind had pushed the boat off the fish mark and I foolishly elected to continue the trawl. Foolish maybe, but everyone does it. All Roughy fishermen think if the trawl is moving then there's a chance of fish, but hauling the net and re-shooting can take hours.

I was invaded by a fear of losing or seriously damaging the trawl gear on the second day of fishing. We retrieved the net gently but we lost some wing-end floats.

When the repairs were completed the young Russian came into the wheelhouse and with a guilty look said we had used up our last spare floats fixing the net. The floats were a deep-water type capable of handling very high pressures [at the time they were worth $400 each].

---

[1] injectable penile erection aid

Stammering involuntarily I said, "We only lost three. I ordered enough for two spare nets".

"Perhaps the engineers are selling them" he replied, which I soon learnt was the excuse for everything.

We headed south scouting for fish on the seamounts along the way. At the 38°30s seamount, there were four vessels: Giuseppe, Newfoundland Lynx, Kermadec, and Arrow working one of the newer tows. It was six hours for a rotation [if no one hooked up]. We booked in with Aussie [Kermadec] who was playing the role of mayor. The mayor allots the order of shooting and keeps the peace with fair-play rulings

Typical "Base Rules of Agreement":-
* Only the boat second in the order can look at the fish mark.
* A boat finishing a trawl must say when his net is clear of the bottom.
* If the next boat doesn't run back to start his tow, then the queue can be jumped.

The rules are stretched with inventive excuses and outright lies. Our six-hour wait lengthened and we guessed some of the boats weren't using fair play. We were being treated like gate crashers, so we moved south to the seamount at 39°s [Jonnies Hill] where we caught a good load the previous year utilizing a dangerous tow.

The Komtek's stock of spare net-bits didn't allow us to go hunting in any risky spots, so I went for a long flat tow and we settled into an around-the-clock towing routine. The crew started demonstrating good teamwork. Catches were small, but product was going in the hold and a full moon was due with a chance of a fish spawn.

A Bit about Moons, Spawns & Storms ○ ○ ○ ○

There are thirteen full moons in a year and at least ten of them arrive with a blow [and /or rain].

Most spawns start after the moon when the tide springs away for the third time.

Most fish will school up and feed before a storm [like the ants that invade the kitchen before bad weather].

The moon came with a storm and we put the ship into *dodge* mode. Waiting out a storm puts another dimension on time. Days become long, barometers are tapped, and weather maps are studied rather than perused. The vessel becomes damp and the walls begin to run with condensation.

This storm was ferocious with a sea that pitched the old vessel skywards and then pounded the under-hull with a bellyflop. Sea-doors and deadlights were dogged, but the rain hit the vessel's sides as if it was shot through water cannon. Water got past weather seals causing slippery companionways and before long the smell of chunder soon started to waft in the stale air.

While the storm raged, it seemed like every seabird in the west Pacific Ocean had joined us. There were thousands of cape pigeons and hundreds of shearwaters, petrels and mollyhawks. Everything with feathers for miles around was floating on our lee side, with albatross claiming the calmest areas. Birds that couldn't hold a position in our lee had to fly and circle back to a free landing area. The bird movement was like a liquid flow.

The soaring, gliding and hovering made a great sight and became a most memorable display of ocean bird aerobatics.

While the small birds put on their synchronized flying displays [at breakneck speed], the albatross swam powerfully in the calm of our lee and vigorously defended their positions by attacking the eyes of the birds that encroached their space.

The storm lasted a week, when the weather improved we

started shooting fish marks for small returns. A couple of days later with no signals indicating fish on our sounder or net monitor, we got a *floater*. The first sign is the water bubbling in shades of blue and white before the bag bursts to the surface. There isn't a better sight to a Roughy fisherman than a big orange sausage floating on the surface behind the stern ramp. It's an exhilarating experience.

With the bag of fish on board, the Russian captain went into a spin. He was having problems comprehending the value of the catch.

He was repeating, "Surely the catch is not worth $125,000. It is a very big astonishment."

We steamed thirty miles off the seamount to process the fish. The separation distance took us outside the radar range of any passing boats and concealed the seabirds feeding on the fish processing offal.

The next two weeks were a mixture of bad weather and small catches. We had been out five weeks and some of the crew had become irritable. Factions began forming and arguing. We held a suspicion that the recent dose of hard work had exposed the slackers. The wheelhouse was getting daily rumble and mumble reports.

Normally, work duties fix grumpy minds and keep a restless crew occupied. The usual tasks are net repairs and cleaning. Our problem was we didn't have enough spares for an orchestrated net demolition, and the cleaning had been continuous since our departure and cleaning duties irritated the crew who weren't willing or experienced at scrubbing anything. It came to a head when the cook scampered into the wheelhouse in a state of alarm.

"He's threatening to kill you. They're going to kill each other and Henrys got a big knife." It was the sort of announcement cooks spread like cheap margarine, although there was a chance it was serious.

I`d seen Henry's knife. The knife was more ornament than implement. It wasn`t a dangerous dirk, it had a hefty haunch, an unsharpened chrome blade and a point that couldn`t puncture a party balloon [or open a letter from the dole office.] If you held it by the blade, it would make a dangerous baton though. All I could say was "Go make some scones." I said it involuntarily as thoughts of mayhem pervaded my mind.

"I'm not going down there. Henry's gone pyschobatic, he's a pyschobates" the cook protested. We had a scared cook and normally it's the cook doing the unnerving. The crew had been watching the movie *Psycho* for days on end and it had spawned words like pyschobatic.

The wheelhouse began buzzing with conversation, but it was interrupted when Pyschobates and another crewman [very large] appeared on the trawl deck and started shaping up at centre-stage. The fighters were two decks below the bridge and from the winch-station windows, you felt like you were watching from balcony seats.

Pyschobatic Henry had his faux-Rambo knife. The other crewman was wielding a pallet-board [complete with rusty-nails]. He swung the timber as if he`d been baseball coached. The combatants were the two largest members of the crew and the action was full of air-shots, threats, and puffing. In fact it looked like big time show-fighting in shoddy clothing.

Danny, the first mate, used the bridge microphone to deliver a hail of abuse over the deck speakers. The intercom volume was tuned to a screeching high level and it stopped the fight in an instant.

Danny grinned, yawned showily, and explained it worked every time. He`d learnt it when he had to control a fighting Tongan crew.

The Russian captain suggested we call a special meeting. We held the meeting in the crews' mess. Constant cleaning had exposed layers of dull multi-coloured paint and it made a dreary backdrop. The crew sat on paint-bare benches with their heads down looking at the pitted floor tiles. They were sitting in two groups with a zone between them. The silence was unnerving, their looks glum, until I spoke, then accusations and arguments boiled in the air.

We tried to calm the situation. Deck knives where taken off some and others had their shifts changed to separate the two protagonists and their followers. The situation about the fish was discussed and they were asked to be patient. I explained that when the next moon came [and the tidal flows strengthened] the fish would be pushed into a better target area. I propounded the theory to promote positivity but no one was interested.

When the fish mark improved, we caught over ten tonnes of fish in quick time. The factory manager was assuming a manner of importance and everyone was busy.

Perhaps the work pressure started it but the fighting started again and this time it was fists, and a good spectacle. The same two big units were swinging punches on a level deck and it was rough with puff. They both landed some big blows with good combinations. Trouble was the villain won. Pyschobates caused a puffed-up eye, a blood-nose, and a scurry.

Pyschobates had scared the insecure and inexperienced crew before his victory, but now he had put the frighteners up them and the cook reported there was talk of mutiny. Our crew were not a mutinous group. They were the product of borstals and work detention gangs with no clues on how to run a boat. They wouldn't even make pirates because they had trouble following orders. They weren't interested in their jobs and every order had to be repeated more than twice.

A delegation of frightened crew lead by one of the more

notable rat-bags arrived in the wheelhouse demanding something be done. They questioned our leadership.

Their accusations made the Russian Captain bristle and he ordered all the crew to write testimonies about the fight. I could see literacy difficulties, but the Captain said "Commander it will fix the situation. If I am wrong, I will shoot myself and you will not need a firing squad."

The crew wrote their witness-statements about the fight. Correct spelling and grammar weren't evident in the testimonies but in three of them, the writers said they feared for their safety. The captain shuffled these statements from the pack.

"This is a safety matter," said the Captain, "Now we have reason to jail the outlaw. It is our duty to protect the vessel and crew from danger."

We locked Pyschobates up in a cabin with an ensuite. Under normal circumstances, it was the owner's cabin, and it was the only cabin with a lock [and a locatable key]. On big boats, the owners cabins are well appointed and have two entries, one a discrete entrance from the deck close to the gangway and the other an internal entrance from a passageway.

The ensuite-cabin wasn't a generous gesture because the toilet back-vent had blocked [or been manipulated by the engineers] and it periodically filled the cabin with eye-watering ammonia fumes from the *black-water* tank [sewage].

Pyschobates went to the cabin peacefully. When we visited him with meals, his head was hanging out the porthole to get fresh air and he didn't seem to care about the occasional dousing with saltwater.

The trip back to New Zealand took over a week and on our arrival in Auckland, the Harbour Authorities made us anchor up outside the harbour. Deep-sea fishing boat owners rarely pay any bills on time and as a result, we were forced to wait overnight at Rangitoto Roads [heart of the Gulf] for the Port Authority to be paid.

While we waited, we made a decision to send Pyschobates ashore in a water-taxi for his safety. The frightened crew were near their hoods and their bravery had increased, loud noises were coming from the lower decks. There was some hot talk doing the rounds [the cook told us].

After Pyschobates departed in the water-taxi, the murmurs died down for a while but then others wanted to go ashore. We were bombarded with excuses and pitiful pleading. Two water-taxis later, half of our crew were ashore. Their actions meant they hadn't completed the voyage and therefore, they weren't eligible for pay.

The next day, what was left of us took the vessel into Auckland. We had achieved eighty-six tows, spent fourteen days dodging bad weather, and unloaded thirty-six tonne of product. Michael rang the boat from Singapore. He wasn't happy with our catch but he offered me a bottle of Scotch as a present. Instead of the grog, I asked him for a kite thinking I could fly it with my grandson whose fourth birthday I'd missed while I was at sea.

I was hoping Singapore might have exotic kites. Dragons or paper birds-of-prey came to mind, but he'd arrived at the boat and presented me with a plastic model looking like it had been purchased at a $2 shop on the way in from Auckland airport.

***

When I got back to Wellington, my grandson was pestering me to fly the kite but Wellington had a rare windless day. I tried to explain the still air wouldn't last long. I mentioned that wind and Wellington were conjoined twins, but the concept of air-mass movement eluded him. It was dead calm for three days, not a cloud in the sky, and without a ripple on the water [or a fairy-seed floating].

Every day the youngster woke me early with the refrain,

"Can we fly the kite today?"

To maintain my *mana*, I took the *mokopuna* to the top of Mount Victoria by the monuments and outlook posts. I told him to run down the hill dragging the kite behind. The kite glided gently behind him while he was running but it plummeted into the tarmac when he turned to look at it.

I tried to explain the importance of an ice cream when waiting for a land-breeze. He ignored me and continued to run down the hill with the same look-back and kite crash finish. It was fun to see his enjoyment and determination.

From the top of '*Mount Vic*' I could see fishing vessels tied up [mostly forever] at the harbours lesser wharves and quays. These vessels hadn't contributed anything to the knowledge of the Louisville Ridge. They had been financed by bankers who had no knowledge of deep-sea fishing trawlers and now they were for sale, tempting another batch of gamblers and dreamers but more likely to be scuttled for artificial reefs.

From the Komteks Internet Record ○ ○ ○ ○

Napier 1998 - Sold

The ex-Russian factory trawler KOMTEK II has been laid up at Napier for a long period. She was sold during Sep 1998 to the same operators who own JAMES COOK (see Vol.47 No.2) [Complete article].

Nelson 2002 - Fire

Source: New Zealand Marine News Reference ID:5101033 Publisher: New Zealand Ship and Marine Society Year2002 Volume51Number1 Page:43 Title: Nautical News: "Komtek II" Author: Pryce, Michael Abstract: Former Russian trawler caught fire 1 Jun 2002 at Nelson. Fire was extinguished in an hour.

Nelson 2003 - Parliament

February 2003 Nick Smith Politician was saying, "My bill, which has been sitting in the ballot for a very long time, would make that plain for vessels like Komtek II, a rust bucket sitting in the Port of Nelson. That vessel has no insurance cover and has a hole in its side. The port company would like to deny it access, but is not lawfully able to do so.

Nelson 2005 - Inland Revenue

On 19th May 2005 a public notice said that Inland Revenue had filed in the High Court on 1st April 2005 to put Szap Overseas Australia Fishing Ltd. Into liquidation. It is understood that they were the registered owners of the trawler SZAP 5 (1,390 gross tonnage, built 1978, ex-KOMTEK II in 2002, ex-OPAL 6 in 1992, ex-KANTEMIR), laid up at Nelson since 10th August 2004.

Nelson 2007 - Scuttling

UPDATE: 29/07/07: Fishing boat leaves port on final trip

The Szap 5, which has been a fixture of Port Nelson since September 2004, has left port on its final trip
.The 59m fishing boat was arrested by the port company in April 2005 for non-payment of berthage back fees and later put up for sale to recover tens of thousands of dollars owed.
Yesterday, it was towed out of Nelson towards a site off Wellington, where it will be scuttled. Port Nelson chief executive Martin Byrne said yesterday that the port company had approval from Maritime New Zealand to sink the ship in waters near Wellington where other vessels had been scuttled.
"We had to get a plan signed off by the authority. We've been planning to scuttle it for some time, but have had to wait for a weather window."
Byrne did not know the exact location of the scuttling, but he understood the Szap 5 would be accessible as a diving wreck. The ship was owned by Tasmanian businessman Harold Adams, and had been berthed in Nelson since September 2004.

SZAP... going ... going ... gone but the court cases carried on and on [for years].

6...Seafire & Xinger

Wellington - April [1999] ₒ ₒ ₒ ₒ

It was a very low tide and the vessel *Seafire* was hanging tight on its lines below Glasgow Wharf, making a descent to the deck impossible. I was level with the Seafires crosstree, standing on a wharf with no rail or ladder. I leaned over the edge with one hand gripping my knee. 'Eyeballing the fall,' they say at Jackson Bay where the berthed boats moved by the swell, shudder the timber-wharf and play with your point of balance.

The act of *calling-down* to a boat at a wharf requires balance and voice-waves sent with laser-point accuracy. It also requires patience on a windy day in Wellington. When calling down to a boat, timing the calls between swells and wind gusts is essential. With the *Seafire* - knowing the breaks in the heavy metal music helped. Calling down to boat is a learnt art, that's needed at all the coastal fishing ports of New Zealand and especially when you're trying to find a party, or borrow some dollars to pay a cab fare.

The *Seafire* always tied up to a wharf, starboard side-to. The crew spaces and mess were on the port side. In the boat's mess and cabins there were extractor fans at work and heavy metal music played loud to counteract the fan noise. Everything worked against you when you were calling down to the *Seafire* and getting a response was just good luck.

The Boston Seafire ₀₀₀₀

The *Boston Seafire* was called Buzzard when it was launched in 1950. It was one of the last of the large side-trawlers and their history is well documented.

Side-trawlers tow nets from one side and the catch comes over the side. On stern-trawlers, the net comes up a stern ramp for added stability and more efficient fish handling.

Boston Seafire ~ Men with bowler hats on poop deck [circa 1950]

Boston Seafire and her sisters are incredible sea boats. They can work a large sea better than any modern stern-ramp vessel and, *by Jove,* give a better sounder-picture than any modern trawler in any loading or weather conditions. She came to New Zealand from Britain where she had been part of the famed Fleetwood fleet. The trawler was called *Seafire* for most of her life and she was the mother boat of NZ Roughy fishing.

She was twenty-four years old and the biggest fishing boat in NZ when she arrived in 1970. She had broken down on the way to NZ and there were court actions when she got here. Those two issues [break down and court cases] set the standard [and tradition] for trawlers arriving from overseas.

74

Wellington - April [1999] o o o o

In 1999, the *Seafire* could no longer be called big in New Zealand. She had become average in size and old in style.

I was yelling down to the *Seafire* as countless others had before me [sometimes you got a response]. It's instinctive to look around for small stones to use as attention-seeking ammunition. Over time, everything had been thrown at the *Seafires* mess-roof, including coins, but I was saved that expense when the crew [Bossy and Tony] appeared on deck. They were the longest serving crew on the *Seafire* in its forty-nine years of fishing.

The pigpen was their kingdom and the rudder-flat held their secrets. They were the crew [and the party], and they had worked a deck responsible for millions of wet socks.

"Was Lindsay on aboard. " I asked, hands cupped to my mouth and using full voice. Lindsey (Elkington) had been the skipper when I was last in Wellington. I was hoping he might know boats with vacancies.

The answer came back that Lindsay had, "Gone fishing in Madagascar." The answer stunned me a bit; it was a big move for a man from D'Urville Island.

Then there was dissension on the deck and after the arguing died down, Mauritius was substituted for Madagascar.

"But it could be some other port in Africa starting with m, who cares." They said in unison

"Sekope was the skipper now." I heard that bit clearly.

Sekopes' diary had been such a great help on the Komtek trip and he was often the subject of conversation on the long nights of sounder watching. Everybody in the Roughy industry had a Sekope story.

He had started as a cadet working the *Boston Seafire* and later skippered the Whitby. He and his fellow skippers gave birth to legend in the early days of fishing off Kaikoura and the

North Island east coast. Sekope had a punch that was feared by all.

It was my luck that the *Seafire* needed a mate for the next trip. "Do you want to fill the position?" asked the ships husband Fat Jack [Pollock] and I was on the crew for saying, "I do."

***

We sailed two days later, heading for the Louisville Ridge, but we were turned around and sent to Lord Howe Rise. Our turn-around meant someone in management was either, winging it or had a cunning plan.

We had kind weather for the whole trip. The *Seafire* was a *wet-deck* boat and it could play in a big seas swell and inspire me to soliloquy...

I've watched Seafire dipping in a rolling sea and shipping water at a measured mass.

I've felt her react with dignity and gently right herself.

I've seen her deck ponds slowly empty through her freeing ports - scuttling water at a measured rate and acting as a stability tank.

I've seen the sea lapping at the topmost edge of her capping rail and I've felt Seafire build up a rhythm of existence the sea could only match.

The exactness of it all gave you unreserved faith in naval architects.

Within four days of arriving at the Challenger Plateau, we found a fish mark and landed twenty tonnes of fish. Fish marks come in different shapes and shades, and they are best described as you see them. One skipper might describe a fish mark as a *grub on the ground* [a greenish mark that looks vaguely like a caterpillar]. This description becomes easily interpreted by another skipper.

When Heals [the doyen of mark callers] once reported a mark looked like *Ma Simpson's hair-do*[1], boats came from miles around having understood his term with clarity.

Scratches, plumes, feathers, rain, haze, dots, and specks are the language of a Roughy hunter reading sounder marks. Roughy normally don't give much of a sounder mark unless they are schooled up in large numbers. Roughy don't have a swim bladder[2], with the pocket of air, which a sounder normally detects. When Roughy are scarce, it is only the aeration from their swim-motion, which shows on the sounder.

We had good catches at the Challenger before wild weather set in and forced us to dodge the storm. During the dodging, we ran over a Roughy mark. Our catches had fish with ripening roes and our mark was typical of a pre-spawn showing. The mark was a small bluish flame and it turned into a hundred metre high plume once a day. The *Seafire's* gentle roll and deep draft gave a perfect sounder picture in the storm conditions.

The fishing ground was a two hundred metre wide boulder-strewn flat behind an eight-mile long ridge. In places there were stacks rising fifty metres above the seafloor. The grounds were a weathered hard edge and needed exact plotting to find safe trawl passages.

Mt Longva was the first fishing seamount discovery [1993] and Chinatown was the last area of discovery [Greg Gallop 1998][3]. Our marks were four miles away from those features and all three areas were connected with range-like spurs.

Our pre-spawn mark disappeared when the weather improved and it was possible it would take a month to come back. We

---

[1] Blue haystack
[2] Roughy have a waxy fluid for buoyancy.
[3] See chart chapter 10

towed Chinatown, a seamount with a reputation for being difficult and we did nothing to harm its reputation. We left a set-of-gear at Chinatown [rotten wire got the blame]. All that came back from the sea floor was a door [portside, if you must know] one bridle and five-and-a-half rows of double mesh hanging on a new hammerlock.

It looked like a bad end and it was, there was no spare door or grapnel on board and we couldn't rig another net or retrieve the lost door. It was the end of the trip. In an instant, our run of good luck had finished, but we did have a pre-spawn mark and it would re-appear somewhere close to where we originally found it.

We docked in Wellington. Sekope said he was going fishing overseas and it seemed everyone of any stature in Orange Roughy fishery had gone fishing in the Indian Ocean.. Fishing berth spaces were empty and the wharves had a new security gate.

The *Seafire* was waiting for trawl gear and wire, but the owners were at the end of their credit lines. A fishing moon was waxing and so was my humour. I was starting to experience a sinking feeling.

When I rang Harry, the ship's manager, [on my new cell phone], he said,

"I'll get back to you" but he didn`t say when, and it would be a first, if he did. But Harry did ring back. It was my first call on my first cell phone and the call answered my undirected prayers.

"Would I like to go on the *Chang Xing* to the Challenger Plateau?" asked Harry.

It was a *'would I?'* occasion and a *no debate* answer. I said *'yes'* and disappointed myself with the meek way I said it. Foolishly, I didn't ask my catch percentage or the departure date. I was in no state to negotiate an employment contract, nor did I care.

The new cell phone was the hero of the day and I still have fond memories of the days of six digit numbers [and Ben Rumble].

Seafire GT 314 LOA 43m at Miramar wharf [2008]
Scuttled 2009 for dive site Whale Island. Bay of Plenty.

Chang Xing 1998. [previous Nororn & Newfoundland Lynx]

Chang Xing - Wellington [1999] ○○○○

The Newfoundland Lynx had been renamed *Chang Xing* and there were other changes. There were new wall-signs, the type that showed dangers and exits. They had been posted beside the existing Norwegian, German and English language notices. The new signs had Chinese calligraphic characters, which looked artistic although how the maritime inspector knew what they portrayed was a bit of a thinking point.

The ship's officers wore matching uniform-jackets and the important crew wore very white overalls. The officers were a smiley bunch who enjoyed singing and the songs filled the air with the smell of their soy-breaths.

Bob [Walford] was the other fisherman and senior partner of our act. Bob had been in the Roughy fishery since the seventies but we had not worked together before. Bob's last fishing trip had been brief when the vessel he was crewing struck Steeple Rock Light before it got out of Wellington harbour. A collision with a lighthouse is a few steps up from being stranded on a sandbar. The lighthouse came off worse although the vessel did need repairs. This unusual incident became fuel for conversation on our outward voyage.

It was a two-day trip out to the Challenger grounds and the Chinese crew did all the net-work needed for the trip. On the way to the grounds, we were made to feel like guests and were treated with respect. We dined at the Captain's table in the company of the Chief Engineer. It was the top table in the mess, which meant the crew had to wait for us to start before they began eating.

On our first night at the top table, the Captain insisted Bob and I start eating first. Bob picked up his chopsticks and demonstrated how adept he was at using them. I am chopstick inept [and fearful], in fact I'm shambolic when I use them, I am a messy eater at the best of times. I should use a napkin for normal dining, but when using chopsticks it would probably be best if I wore my wet weather gear.

The ships mess was a full house and I saw nothing but the crews' eyes staring at me as I hesitated to pick up the *hashi sticks*. I glanced towards the galley and the cook [without any prompting] quickly brought me a knife and fork. It was at this moment when I got my first smiles from the crew [and I felt they were close to applauding]. The crew weren't permitted to leave the mess until we had finished eating, which might have caused the grinning [and silent applause.]

A bit about Orange Roughy ₒ ₒ ₒ ₒ

Roughy, like most ocean fish, don't spawn in exactly the same place every year. The shift is normally no more than five nautical miles and there is a good chance they will feed at the same depth. Normally Roughy require a feature [rock or gully] to aid the spawn fertilization and egg distribution. A food source is never far away. Often the feature is the highest point in their habitat range. A Roughy fisherman spends hour upon hour plotting out the rocks and noting their exact height and position. Sometimes these rocks *grow* when fish lump up on top of them or the fish might mimic a rock on a sounder display or a rock might look like fish.

Challenger Plateaux - [1999] ₒ ₒ ₒ ₒ

When we arrived at the Challenger Plateau the deep-sea vessels *Baldur, Clarabelle, Atlantic Elizabeth, Saxo Anglo, Ocean Ranger, Waipori, Nan Hai* [and a couple of others my lazy memory conceals] were shooting the seamounts. All the vessels had been at the South Tasman Rise [south of Tasmania] where they had enjoyed good catches. They were taking turns at *bombing* the local seamounts and doing little else. It was a lazy pod of trawlers with the patience to wait.

We used the time between our shots to circle back to the starting position, looking for the spawn marks found on the

Seafire trip. We hunted around the clock and within forty-eight hours, it was BINGO with capitals. We found our Roughy spawn plume of fish ninety metres high. The mark looked big enough to fill all seven boats, but we didn't feel like sharing and knew the fish would hang around for a month if left undisturbed. We started going over the fish-mark using deceptive courses.

The plotters and radars on a typical Roughy boat are interfaced to record the target tracks as an overlay. These tracks supply information about course, position, and speed. We were plotting all the vessels around us out to twenty nautical miles using the ARPA function on the *war-toy* radar. It was clear from the plotting we hadn't given the fish mark away. Other boats were just going back to the starting area between trawl shots and not searching the surrounds.

The problem with factory boats is they are a dead giveaway when they are catching fish. On factory boats, the offal from processing goes over the side. It can be stopped for a while, but eventually it has to be released. The waste attracts everything with wings, flippers, fins, and nets. Fifteen minutes after the discharge begins up to a thousand sea birds will be gathered, fighting around the stern and making it hard to lie about your catch.

We started the fishing phase of a Roughy spawn. The stakes were high. Catches are worth millions of dollars to the boat owners and hundreds of thousands of dollars in catch shares to the crew and officers. A successful harvest with other boats in close proximity requires towering heights of slipperiness, cunning, and guile. It turns a wheelhouse into a den of deviousness.

What is normally needed, at these times, is a collaborator to help split the other vessels up and drag as many as possible away from the scene of the action by using lies and misinformation. The best you can hope for [but it happens rarely] is another boat to find spawn-fish a good distance off and leave you to it.

Bob and I were friendless. The other vessels had worked out alliances and information sharing before the season began. We had been the last boat to get ready and we were the last boat to arrive. It didn't help we were a foreign crewed vessel and the biggest boat. Outside fishing, Bob and I weren't close pals with any of the other skippers either.

We had an advantage because we found fish at the time the Roughy were *doing it*. It was an easy decision to give the spawn spot a rest from our sounder signals. There are popular theories the sounder signals can disturb the fish, although most indications would suggest they are unmovable at spawn time.

Deep-sea trawlers have several VHF radios so they can monitor the distress channel [channel 16] while they are using general working channels for chitchat. When preseason alliances are formed, there is agreement on secret channels.

There are dozens of channels, so monitoring the lot [and getting a result] is a long shot, even with automatic scanning facilities. Secret channels can be devious. On a simple level, forgotten CB radio communications can be used. On a sneaky level, the high frequency [UHF/SSB] radiotelephone channels with different receive and transmit frequencies are used.

We were getting radio call ups. Normally a busy radio means fish are scarce and the caller is dealing with boredom. Sometimes the calls are an attempt to find out who is on watch and by deduction ascertain the boats state of readiness. The main fisherman will do his watch at the more likely times.

While we searched and plotted, Bob was chatting on the VHF radio to all [and sundry] in an everyday sort of way. His clash with the lighthouse made good diversionary chat and brought out some good humour. His slow delivery and low tone helped to disguise our eagerness to have a trawl the other boats couldn't detect. On one of these occasions, after chatting with another vessel, fortune favoured us when the radio wasn't turned back to its usual monitoring channel, and it was on channel 88A which meant we were left earwigging a very private conversation regarding the state of the play.

Two of the senior skippers working for the largest company were talking. Their conversation filled in every gap and answered our doubts about being watched while we tracked the fish.

One said he thought there were too many boats bombing the Chinatown seamount and he didn't think anything would happen until it got a rest.

The other said he needed some downtime because his hydraulics needed repairs. He indicated he was heading for Mount Easy [nine hours away] where he had seen fish sign earlier in his trip and he was going to check on 'the Irishman' [Brendan] who was over there and being a bit quiet.

The other skipper wondered if anyone was talking to the big one.

We were `the big one` and the comment made us turn our radio receiver volume up and point our ears [stretched beyond normal size] at the radios speaker. "Not that I know of but I can't be sure about the Lizzie was the answer.

The Lizzie [*Atlantic Elizabeth*] was owned by Seafresh who were managing our charter. Wizza [the skipper] wasn't the type to give fish to anyone and certainly not to a bigger boat.

"They didn't tell them last year," was the reply then he came over channel 16 cancelling his position in the shooting order, *"We're pulling out to do maintenance and check some other seamounts."*

Immediately other boats joined the exodus using various excuses and we couldn't help thinking they heard about fish being caught down the track. The defections left four boats. This lessened the time between shots and meant the remaining boats were fully occupied and less likely to see our deceptions.

We did fishing feints and made a pass over the ninety-metre plume at midnight. The fish were 'down', meaning the school reached to the seafloor and it was easy to get a net through them for a good catch.

The next night, after our tow, we lied about a ripped net and steered a straight course to the plume. The fish were there and the mark looked better than the night before. At 0245 hours, the *Lizzie*, a diamond on our plotter, not only went close to the plotted position of our fish plume but it went back a mile-and-a-half, turned, and slowed to trawl speed. When the graphic interface showed they had finished trawling, we sent Wizza a satellite-fax simply asking, 'Any fish?'

No reply ... four hours later no reply ... they hadn't been near the mark up until then and it was obvious they had plotted and sussed our movements. The lack of response to our query suggested they were hard at it, icing fish in their hold.

Mid-morning, we called them on the VHF radio with a "Did you get our sat-fax?" inquiry. "Yes" said the mate Mark [Hansen] and he added that Wizza would get back to us after he finished sleeping.

"Don't try and wake him," we chortled in unison. Both Bob and I had worked with Wizza and we knew he slept as if he was in deep hibernation. Waking Wizza was never an easy task.

When Wizza replied a few hours later, it was by sat-fax and there was an air of panic in his message.

> O There's a mountain of fish - enough for both of us.
> O We got some fish out of it last night. Don't let the others know.
> O We can both get a load. Confuse the bastards _ www

Wang [the interpreter], was vetting all our in-mail and looked amused when he handed the message over. Wang was an academic type, and not like the other Chinese crew who were obvious sea dogs. We brought up the sounder memory on the screen and showed him our fish mark and we remarked "Mountain of fish!" but he wasn't interested nor did he bother to translate the details to the wheelhouse officers.

We replied to Wizza...

o   Give it a day or so - We'll stay mum
o   The others don't know anything
o   We heard them talking on their secret channel _ Ajaski

We now had an alliance with Wizza but he was known to be duplicitous and it started a period of the high anxiety which started us scratching at excitement rashes. Later Wizza swore he had worn his teeth down through chewing his fingernails out; Bob got an acute attack of gout [although he blamed the Chinese food] and I obsessed about weather patterns, hoping we weren't stormed out.

Finally, Bob could wait no longer. He reckoned it would take the other boats a couple of days to twig us, but he was driven by greed and an impending marriage.

`About to tow`, we lied in a sat-fax to the Lizzie. The net had already been slipped off the deck and we shot it in the dark, with the deck and factory lights switched off to hide the activity. The Chinese thought working in the dark was amusing.

We aimed to get a smallish bag, up to thirty tonnes of fish to start the factory cycle and follow it up with a big bag, then go about our processing well away from the action and out of radar range. Managing to land a small catch is not an easy task when there's a mountain of fish involved. Although we got close the factory needed an hour to clear the deck before we could shoot the nets again.

While we trawled, Wizza 'cooked up a storm'. He accused another boat of dangerously cutting him off and not obeying the Maritime Rules. The accusation broke the accused anger control and before long they were arguing [with threats] in a very public way. It was a major distraction and the most primitive of decoys, but it worked.

We sent Wizza a fax telling him we were going again in about an hour and we added the details

> O   Towing 165° True. Keeping gear light all over the place.
> O   Fish best midnight until 0230 hour _Xinger
> O

We towed again for thirty tonnes making fifty tonnes on-board. Processing the catch would take over twenty-four hours. The work had the Chinese crew singing.

We named the knob [982 metres deep] *Xinger* after the *Chang Xing* but it didn't mean anything to the Chinese. The spawn-plume might be seen once a year, [if you were lucky], but they didn't understand the rarity of it.

Our plotter track showed the Lizzie moving into trawl the plume. The Lizzie was an ice-boat [no factory] and it was capable of putting a hundred tonnes of fish on ice [while we processing thirty tonne to frozen blocks] and still beating us to the next tow. The next night we got another large bag of Roughy, but the game was up by then as the other boats worked out we were in harvest mode.

It didn't take long before there were vessels, horizon-wide. The radio became busy with people booking in and relaying tow angles. An order came through from Seafresh [our charter company] that we were to help the *Nan Hai* [skipper Goose] with fishing information.

Wang [the interpreter] hadn't looked happy when he passed the message over. The two Chinese-crewed boats were rivals and the crew were from cities on opposed peninsulas, separated by an eighty-mile strait, on the seaway to the Yellow Sea. We were on a vessel, with a Chinese crew from Dalian, and our crew kicked up a fuss every time the *Nan Hai* [from Yantai] passed by.

Our bridge officers and crew put on a display directed at the passing *Nan Hai*. Actually, they gave a riveting professional performance. It was a display of neighbourly disgust like a hissing haka. There were no words, but there was thigh slapping, foot stomping, chest beating, and face pulling. It was a spectacular display three-decks-high if you counted the factory workers shaking gloves out of the lower level portholes!

There's a big relief when *secret fish* are finally out in the open, but it is also a time when a new crop of mind games are required. Paul [Hendry] likes to say, "The only time you know a fisherman is telling the truth is when he calls another fisherman a liar". Alliances lie to each other and skippers use cunning to slot into trawl times when planning a day ahead.

The *Lizzie* filled up and everyone else '*got a feed*' as they say about a better than average pay. We finished up with seventy tonnes of product and headed to Wellington to store up for a trip to the Louisville Ridge. It was good pay for two weeks work.

Bob didn't want to do a trip to the Ridge as he was about to get married. Management said, "Get married when you get back. Have it at our restaurant." They smothered him with compliments and inducements, but Bob held his ground.

Stu [Langridge] jumped at the job – he had been one of the early skippers when the vessel was the Newfoundland Lynx. We had been a successful wheelhouse team on earlier occasions.

***

Wellington - June [1999] ₒ ₒ ₒ ₒ

Before we sailed to the Louisville Ridge there were a couple of days to fill-in while the ship was unloaded and provedored. I visited Geoff [Cochrane], a friend who has worked as a poet and author with recognition but little reward. We are a two-man cigarette smoking-club, and during this visit, he offered me a book written by John Steinbeck. He was sure few people had read it.

Over the years, the books that Geoff recommended have become my favourite reads and Melville's *Bartleby the Scrivener- A story of Wall Street*, is always the first to spring to mind I put Geoff's book offering, The *Log from the Sea of Cortez* in my sea bag. It was a change from the *Cruise of the Cachalot,* which seemed to be the first-choice book-gift for departing deep-sea fishermen.

In mid-June 1999, we sailed for the Louisville Ridge. We had been fishing the Louisville Ridge for five years, but 1999 was the year of new discoveries. Places, we previously thought were of no interest became spawning grounds. t was also the year of a new influx of skippers. They had been mates and off siders in previous years, and brought a new vigour to the Ridge with their fresh ideas and hunches.

It was a five-day trip to the Ridge and the Chinese crew did the watches. I started reading *The log from the Sea of Cortez*. Steinbeck wrote of his adoration of Ed Ricketts and his love of things marine.

I drew a comparison with Surge and the Conger project. Steinbeck and Ricketts were collecting shellfish for science labs, schools, and museums. Their activities would send Surge into frenzy if he got wind of it. *'Men really do need sea-monsters in their personal oceans,'* wrote Steinbeck in a quotable way.

Through the Steinbeck book, I discovered *atavism* and the existence of hind legs on whales. Steinbeck thought atavism was the reason people go fishing. He tried to explain how the fishing trip on the *Western Flyer* isolated him from the human world – it was 1940 and World War II had begun while he was away at sea. He caught snatches of news every time he went ashore and understood America would enter the conflict. Isolation and internalization are hard to explain because they are so personal, but the book was a great diversion for the five-day trip.

We started fishing at the Thirty-eight-thirty seamount and it produced fish from the first tow. During our second day at the seamount, we got a message from Karl [Hoggarth] on the *Atlantic Elizabeth* urging us to come to the Capetown Seamount. His fax said '*allez-allez*' and we were on our way despite the fact we had caught twenty tonne of fish that day. Karl's information could always be trusted. The trip south was 280 miles in a straight line and over a day with full steam and calm sea.

When we arrived at the Capetown seamount, the *Lizzie* was still there. Normally a boat is only called in when there's one bag to go and often the call comes when the informant is on the way into port. The fish mark was there too and the fish were forming on a headland rock near the summit of the seamount making it a relatively easy trawl.

We were quickly into factory mode and landing good catches with regularity until there was a loud noise from the deck. The sounded vibrated throughout the vessel. It was the sound of something mechanical breaking in a big way and it put the auto-trawl into confusion. The auto-trawl control was cranking and paying wire with random abandonment.

The smell from the overworked winch-brakes permeated the gloom in the wheelhouse. A winch investigation revealed a broken 100mm diameter stub-shaft. The shaft had broken before. The last time it had taken a fortnight to machine another one. It was expensive to fix. It was a big undertaking getting all three thousand metres of wire back from the deep using only one trawl drum.

Our satellite communications were busy during the thirty-six hours it took to retrieve the gear. With the gear on board, the winch was pulled down and the shaft extracted. The broken shaft had sheered and the break faces were crystalline and geographic. Engineers, experts and the overly opinionated agreed the sheer-point needed some sort of stabilization and reinforcing. First of all the land-based amongst them needed to see the drawings.

All big boats carry a set of drawings on-board. They are voluminous and often notated in a foreign language. There are hundreds of drawings and as many reference guides. The detail plan of the winch shaft arrangement was located under a seat in the Chief Engineers cabin.

The chief's cabin had storage seats around the walls and they were full of plans. By the time the right blueprint was located his cabin looked like a lawyer's office. The drawings had cardboard covers with brass fasteners and German labels. Interpreter [Wang] could read German, but his skills turned him into an arrogant obstructionist when it came to repairs. The breakdown had given him a chance to be omnipotent. He translated the plan annotations into both Chinese and English!

Each folder looked like it held dozens of drawings. The contents were a great example of how many times you can fold a sheet of *Emperor*[1] drawing paper and reduce it to foolscap size. The plans were folded concertina-like. Unfolding them took a minute and refolding them started awkward smiles from

---

[1] Large sheet size 183x122 cm (72 x 48 inches).

frustration and embarrassment. The *stub-shaft plan* was drawn to real scale [1:1] so it could be used as a pattern. This caused a problem because there was no way to fax it and maintain its integrity. The fax attempts led to frustration [Chinese] and argument.

During our time on the *Chang Xing,* it had become obvious the crew had useful secondary skills. We saw a fish kicker double as a mirror welder; a galley hand who became the barber of choice for the captain and crew; and a deckhand who was the boat's electronics genius.

To solve the fax transmission problem a factory hand was tasked to draft the sheet of engineering drawings down to A4 size with overlapping margins and joining edges. He was allotted the chief engineers dayroom to work in. When I looked in on him, he was using a cheap household ruler and HB pencil. His drafting was clear, precise work, to perfect scale.

I always packed a pencil case when I went to sea. The kit contained a scale ruler and needle-thick drawing pens for correcting maritime charts. I took my pencil case and scale rules to the dayroom thinking they might help the draftsman.

The case had fiberglass erasers and masks as well as expensive clutch pencils with graphite leads [hard, medium and soft]. It had flexible curves and more, but the only thing he wanted was my small pencil-knife. He grinned and opened its stainless-steel blade then sharpened his pencil to a perfect point.

He picked up the plastic pencil sharpener he had been using and shook his head. I watched him work for an hour. I was fascinated by his draughtsmanship, but was surprised [shocked!] when he asked me [with language difficulties] if I had any dirty books.

Port Wellington - Late July [1999] ○ ○ ○ ○

The pilot came aboard outside the heads and started going about the pilotage business of ordering courses down the harbour leads. He asked if any of the bridge officers spoke English and we pointed to Wang and explained he could speak good English, French, and German.

Obviously, the pilot had his fill of foreign crews that week. as he said loudly in a P and O sort of pommy way "Gad, they don't just speak one language they speak a dozen."

The statement could have provoked an international incident as it had been said loud enough. Wang looked at me and beckoned me into the radio room. I left the pilot and followed Wang into the small office. He hadn't heard the remarks; he had problems of his own. He had been assigned to tea making! Such is the interpreter's lot when harbour manoeuvres are being undertaken by the mariners.

"Please," he said meekly. "I asked the pilot if he would like a cup of tea and he said, "Just milk. What does he want?"

"He means no sugar" I replied without thought. Wang had been an obstructionist the whole trip and on this occasion, I had missed an opportunity for payback and I kicked myself for quite a long time afterwards.

7...Santa Monica & Article 7

Wellington - February [2000] o o o o

A large noisy mobile crane was lifting blocks of fish through the deck-hatch and shifting them to the wharf. Itinerant workers, in ragged wet-weather gear, shifted the blocks displaying toilers' temperaments and obvious discomfort.

The unload gang [Team John Adams] lumped the frozen fish blocks [20°c below] from cargo nets to pallets. A forklift shifted the pallets into shipping containers. They had been hard at it since dawn. Shifting the 3000 blocks of Roughy product from the bottom holds was wet work in a cold, noisy environment.

A Ministry of Fisheries observer was counting the frozen blocks and checking the unload weights. Marty [Alasker] and I were supervising the unloading although Alasker spent most of his time child minding.

About the Santa Monica and Flat Towing o o o o

The boat was the *Santa Monica*. The ex-Japanese research vessel had paperwork verifying it had been built to handle typhoons, the self-fuelling revolving storms that are called hurricanes or cyclones in other parts of the world.

The *Monica's* design was from the *In-submersible School of Fishing-vessel Architecture*. It had no useful portholes, and the only egress was through two heavy watertight doors.

Santa Monica : LOA 39.67m 379 GT 956 kW

Flat towing gives the crew time to relax. A trawl can take up to three hours and sometimes longer 'if the catches are lean and the skipper not so keen'.

Pinnacle fishing is hectic; it involves setting a boat in storm conditions and landing a net on an area as big as a helicopter-pad [at eight hundred metres depth]. The gear must be hauled out, at an exact moment, to catch the fish and avoid the hook-up from hell. Pinnacle fishing is a story of lost and wrecked nets.

Getting a *fast'ner* on the flats isn't a big deal [normally]. Unhooking it can be done at a casual pace and any damage done requires minimal net mending. The major problem with flat towing is the by-catch. The by-catch is a collection of exotic jellyfish, waterlogged logs, starfish and worthless unwanted fish species. The by-catch slows the tow; the jellies and starfish fill the meshes and their removal from the catch takes up valuable time.

Flat trawling is the subject of condemnation by environmental groups but it has contributed immensely to the knowledge of fish habits, species variations and habitat.

By-catch creatures are discarded back to the ocean. Starfish and Jellies carry on with their lives, while the worthless unwanted fish become prawn tucker. Pinnacle fishing is target species only, whereas bottom-tow fishing can produce surprises.

Marty and the Big Shark ₒ ₒ ₒ ₒ

It was around noon when a monster shark appeared [tail first] through the deck-hatch. We rigged all our block-and-tackles to get the awkward deadweight into the fish-hold. It came out easy [pulled against the sharks-skin grain] using the mobile crane and a long strop. I will never forget the look of triumph on the faces of the unloading gang.

The shark had been caught while we were working the flat areas at the Challenger Plateau. When the shark was landed, there had been a lot of sweating and swearing just getting it out of the net. Then the photo opportunities became good fun. The crew took turns lying full length along its gutted stomach with their grinning heads stuck out where its arse had been. They pushed a pair of gumboots into its mouth. The backdrop was a deck of shark blood.

When we first saw the big shark, it had been a *high-on-the-scale* surprise, but an equally large surprise was the fact Marty [Alasker] had never seen one before.

When the shark first came aboard, he proclaimed loudly, "I've never seen anything like it - look at those squinty eyes!

"Beware of anything that squints", he warned with narrowed eyes.

Just being there, when Marty saw something for the first time, was considered by some of us to be a lifetime achievement. Marty had been home-schooled [on a fishing boat] by his adventurer father and had a fish knowledge which was truly remarkable.

Marty normally worked the line-fishery and his friendship with Skipper Heals got him the job on our trawler. He was hard working and good company at sea, but he had a habit of moving on just when others started to rely on him. That Alasker, a line fisherman, a skilled and flamboyant snood-handler had considered work on a trawler said a lot about his latest love interest [who lived in Wellington].

Marty had been waiting for the shark to be unloaded. He'd been quayside for three hours with five kids [6 to 13 years: three boys, two girls]. They were the issue of his latest flame and whanau. The children were not behaving well, which led us to discussions on Genghis Khans grandkids. They jettisoned the vessel's loose dunnage. We considered 'jettisoning' might be genetic behaviour; such was their need to throw things overboard.

Two boxes of lead pencils, normally used for navigational work had disappeared along with a ream of copy paper. The kids used the paper to make darts [paper wings and pencil fuselages] and the planes ended up floating over the surface of the harbour. Together, the kids had caused the chief engineer to lock himself in the engine room and the ship's owners to leave the vicinity in a scurry. The kids were a reason why people go to sea.

Marty tried to control them but with little effect. They had shut down the boat's computer system with keyboard vandalism and set off alarms without effort. Eventually we banished the horde to the wharf [Aotea Quay] where the older brats completely cleared the topsides by throwing everything they could lift or shift into the harbour basin.

The little monsters publicly exposed Marty's weak points [previously unknown to us] to obtain sweets, ice creams, soft drinks, T-shirts and fries. He had told them to be patient close to a hundred times before the plum-coloured[1] leviathan came into sight. The shark stopped the brats in their tracks and made the unload-gang stop work and gawk. The kids started asking individually, "What sort-of a shark is it?"

The gutted shark on deck.

Marty was letting out loud sighs and repeatedly told them the fisheries officer will tell us soon, but the questions keep coming.

"Is it a man eater?" asked the boy with a growing-out mullet cut.

"How big are its teeth?" asked the thumb sucker.

"Where are its eyes?" asked the one with glasses, hugging a skateboard.

"Why are they called sharks?" asked the girl wearing a dirty pink tracksuit.

"How come it's got slime all over it?" asked the nerdish brat who had a chest-pocket full of the ships paper clips.

---

[1] Some would say it was aubergine coloured.

"What do they do with the dead fish?" asked the five-year-old thumb sucker with seriousness.

"They cook it," answered Marty, "It's the fish you have with your chips."

"How much does it weigh?" asked the nerd and then the youngest child wanted to know if they could have fish and chips tonight. The questions kept coming...

"Did you catch it with a big hook?"

"Can we take it home to show Mum?"

Marty was looking content. "We caught it in the net." Marty answered and added, "No, we are not taking it home."

The shark with a heavy chain-strop around its thick tail had landed on the wharf surface and spread out [blobbed] without grace. Its skin was almost a fur and it had two small seal-like dorsal fins. The fisheries officer measured it and declared it was 5.4 metres overall.

Marty tried to organize the kids for a photo but they kept asking, "What sort of shark is it Marty?"

He grinned to the greasy max and sighed out load, "I bet it's not a card shark or a pool shark. The fisheries officer will tell us its name soon."

He teased the kids, "It might be a Creepy Shark." He cackled while waggling his fingers witchy-like at the younger kids and it got them squirming.

He confided he was high on just having something to show the kids and having them 'sort-of' listen to him. He had an awkward but pleasant way of handling the kids who would test the sanity of most people. His easy nature was also his edge at sea. The secret to looking after the kids, he said, was to act like a shepherd's eye-dog and keep them where you could see them all – never mind the carnage. Just watching them raised my blood pressure, but high blood pressure was never one of Marty's problems.

The Fisheries officer finished thumbing through his fish books and he gave Marty a note with the scientific and common names for the shark. He adjusted his glasses and said "Gurry Shark?" Talking fish, Marty's reaction was like a *stunned mullet*. His lips moved as he read the name or the shark, while his face dropped out of its usual grin. His calm demeanour had been pricked. The written word had done what the delinquent kids couldn't.

He let out a tirade "We lug it to the ice-hold avoiding hernias and snapped tendons and when I get home, I'm chuffed. I tell the kids and everybody else who listens about the monster shark we've caught. Yes, they will be able to see it, and yes, they can have their photos taken with it".

"I'll tell you what they say". They say, *what sort of shark is it?*" [His voice had gone loud and the kids had gone into a momentary safety-cluster].

"I've had twenty four hours of them asking, '*what sort of shark is it?*' He flashed them a quick smile and a wink – he was upset and angry but not out of control. "I don't know what sort of shark it is but I tell them it weighs more than a tonne."

"We gutted the shark and the liver took up four fish-cases at 40 kg each" he drew breath "That's a lot of liver!" Blood flushed Marty's face and puffed it up.

"Only an ichthyologist fisholigist-scientologist could call a shark with no eyes and looks like a huge interplanetary torpedo a Gurry Shark!"

"Guppy sounds more menacing than Gurry". "What's a Gurry? Look at those squinty eyes will you. How could they call it a Gurry?" Marty was asking questions to nobody in particular; secretly he'd hoped the shark had a power name. His pick was *Great Pulse-Hunter Shark* but he knew, if that was its name, he would have heard of it.

A bit of Marty that was attractive in an odd way, was the way he could go on association-raves. On those occasions, the rest of us just enjoyed the humour involved.

"You can see it's different from other sharks," he was dealing with mental issues. I know Great Squinty-eyed Shark doesn`t sound much and it was probably the first name discarded, when it came to naming it.

"They named *Albino Walking fish*, they named *Black-eyed Thicklip fish* and they had *Red eye wrasse* and *Blind eels* - so why was squinty eyed shark was off the christening list".

"There were Gurrys in the book *Moby Dick*" said the Ministry man but Marty totally ignored the comment.

"I know they can't all be called Tiger sharks," Marty said shaking his head and catching his breath for a nano-second of silence before ranting on, "We catch a monster from the deep and it has super squinty-eyes. You would have thought its name was an easy guess. It should have been easy. Anyone can see it has Squinty eyes."

"Strabismus means squinty." The Ministry man suggested when Marty took breath, "I remember there was a Dr Strabismus in a comedy show." The Ministry man straightened his glasses again and said "*Strabazein* would have been a good name for the shark."

Marty thought it was a clever comment but he carried on... "Sharks are all eye." He was away on a tangent and interruptions wouldn`t lip-trip him.

"Sharks eyes are banquet-plate size with a wiper mechanism." He was imploring with pauses, "When sharks look at you, it's all eye contact and they make you feel like a menu item. Big sharks check out the space at the back of your brain. Their gaze is like an optometrist's inspection. These sharks squint at you, through slits, like security cameras or those things that work traffic lights."

He stopped raving to tell the kids the Sharks name, "It's a Gurry Shark kids like the famous ones in the book *Moby Dick the White Whale*."

The MAF observer sidled up to him again and said, "Marty it's also known as a Pacific Sleeper Shark."

"That's a worse name than Gurry, why couldn't the fish-namers come up with anything more dramatically impressive for these monsters?" Marty was off again.

"What's wrong with Stealth or Sonar for a name? Big starts with capital B, why not Batholithic or Biosonar, take your pick, even Ballistic would have worked."

"They could have called it the Sneaky Stealthy Shark, something as big deserves a power name with humour."

The Alasker rave was in progress, he wouldn't stop and he had a captive audience.

"Snakes have the power names Pit Vipers, Death Adders, Asps, Black Mambos, Cobras," he raved, to justify something to himself and he went on, "What have sharks got, White Pointers, Black Tipped, and Basking."

He would have remonstrated in a big way. He was working up to it, but his arms were full of children's clothes and his free fingers had the piece of paper with, *Gurry Shark ~ Pacific Sleeper ~ Somniosus Pacificusi*, written on it. The Observer suggested the sharks closed eyes probably gave it the name Sleeper.

Marty was having none of it, "The shark wasn't sleeping, its eyes weren't closed, they were squinting. You have to open your eyes to see the difference." His little joke did him good.

He was at once the Marty of old and it showed. Shoulders back and chin out he anticipated the children's next question and after a loud sigh, he told the brood.

"Kids, the shark is also known as the Pacific Sleeper Shark and no, it wasn't sleeping when we caught it."

"I thought it was a proper shark," the nerd kid said loud and clear.

The sharks name had deflated Marty, but it didn't worry the kids because the Chief Engineer [Ned] had given them bits of wood and they were busy propping jaws and prising eyes. Oddly, the eye probing looked like civilised behaviour.

The six-year-old child had a last question though; he wanted to know why it was porple?

"You can't say purple properly," said the nerd kid [once again, he was loud and clear] and that started an argument [with tears]. When Marty's mob left the scene, they were still arguing about how to say purple and we started making a list to replace the stationery.

The shark was the biggest by-catch any of us had seen and a bit of an omen for the trip ahead. We were headed for International Waters at the South Tasman Rise, 200 sea miles below Tasmania.

Surge, [Millennium Annual Report] o o o o

Surge was in touch with what he was calling *'the annual report, millennium edition'* and he hinted he was cruising through life and his marriage was back on track. He had a bonanza catch of Congers in the summer season and a good local market.

"Now there's nothing in the holding pot and I'm drinking bottled beer and smoking small cigars. We are debt free. Everything's paid for including the spare gear and it only took six years." The way he said it, you could sense pride and irony.

He complained he hadn't done any conger catching lately [that had probably helped his marriage] because he *'didn't feel like doing it alone'*. His nephew [Tai] had been helping but there had been an accident with a big conger. The nephew's thumb was swallowed by an eel and Surge made a medical mess trying to get it out of the congers jaw. His lowered voice suggested he was still dealing with the mishap and his actions.

"His thumb never recovered from the trauma and it's buggered his guitar playing even though it looks like a strummer. Actually it looks a bit like a ducks bill but he complains it's too painful to play and he can't hold a pick."

The deckhand accidents didn't finish there but Surge's mood turned away from serious, he chuckled loudly before he told his latest *blood and congers* story. It was about Darcy [the architect] who had been helping on a trip after his nephew went back to Thames.

"Darcy picked up a big Conger by the back of the gills, but the conger flicked its tail up and whopped him. The tail hit Darcy's glasses and broke his nose below the bridge. The shattered glass from the lenses cut his cheeks and eyebrows."

"There was blood everywhere and it's still all over the dingy.". Surge gave a thorough accident report.

"I've been in the midst of a Ministry mail-bombardment," he said with an affectation which made him sound like a war reporter. "These days the mail comes in rubber banded bundles. There's letters from ACC, DoL, OSH, DSW, and other Government Departments. I never dreamed of so much mail when I built the letter box and now it can't handle the loading."

He told how the rural postage contractor now drives the kilometre down his track and delivers the mail to the door and they joke about what a couple of Congers can do.

Surge suggested I make a Conger visit and his prompt had hit my guilt-nerve [on the raw-end]. I told him I was off to

Tasmania but I would catch up after the Roughy season and then I had added, "I'll tell you about the Sleeper Shark we caught."

South Tasman Rise [STR] ₀ ₀ ₀ ₀

Our trip across the Tasman Sea in late March had few incidents. We had a full complement of ten on board including the Fisheries Observer [Justine]. Wood End Lighthouse and Farewell Spit passed by with a Dolphin visit. We crossed the twelve hundred miles of the South Tasman Sea without any sightings of vessels [or containers adrift and full of rum].

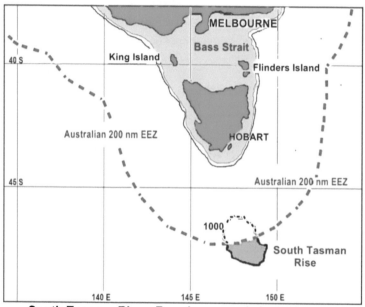

South Tasman Rise - Roughy ground shown orange.

There were three boats fishing at the STR when we got there, the *Cape Hood* and *Whitby*[1] with Hobart homeports and the

---

[1] The Whitby had a long history in the Nelson fishery

Ocean Ranger from Nelson, [and all the vessels had NZ skippers]. The seamount they were working was a typical Roughy feature. It was a high headland on a large undersea plateau.

The seamount was eight hundred and fifty metres below sea level and had been fished for years with varying results. In 1999, it produced a bumper catch harvested by licensed boats from both sides of the Tasman and pirates from South Africa.

Our initial trawl shots produced a few Roughy but the catch was Black Shark and Rat-tails [and too many of them]. Normally the '*blacks and rats*' are the first fish to appear when spawning activity is finished. It didn't look good – our arrival timing had been in line with the previous spawns but the skippers of the other boats reported there hadn't been any spawn activity. They were all known liars and it made the situation unclear.

Our factory manager [Muzzy] came into the wheelhouse wanting to know if we were going to process the Black Sharks. Justine, the MAF observer, inquired whether we had read Article 7 in our fishing permit. The Ministry of Fisheries contract permit hadn't changed in years and we had become lazy checking it, even though the first clause stated "The licensee should be familiar with all the clauses etc."

Justine, had asked, when she did her pre-ops checks, if we had read the contract and skipper Heals had answered, '*yes*', in a manner that suggested '*of course*'. Now she was asking if we had read Article 7, and were we aware we had to return to New Zealand with everything we caught.

"Everything's a big word," said Heals as he came out of his skipper's corner and got set for an argument.

"The Coral and rocks have to be returned to the seafloor" said Justine, who was unfazed by his utterance. Skipper Heals interjected again "What coral? – have you seen any coral?"

Justine continued "All fish and shellfish have to be

unloaded in NZ." Justine offered an opened contract fluoro-highlighted at Article 7.

"What shellfish? Have you seen any shellfish?" roared Heals.

Justine had good people skills and she needed them. Skipper Heals was getting agitated and used the word *malarkey* more than once. The *playboy-granny* tattooed on his monstrous left calf started showing angry eyes and doing bodybuilding exercises.

Discussion on Article 7 continued and it was fed by satellite-fax and radiophone. It was obvious our management hadn't been aware of the clause or its implications. You couldn't help thinking about what our fishmonger masters would do with the by-catch. Would it be turned into a potent fertilizer or might the domesticated city-cats get a little less quality in their cans of gourmet fish.

The article 7 problem got the crew gloomy, which spread an unhappy mood throughout the boat. When you're not catching fish and the boat is spending long periods sitting out storms, *Waid-H*[1] virus symptoms become apparent. The situation was saved when the Chief Engineer [John] was caught pumping up our cook while she sat on the washing machine with the spin cycle turned to the max. The act produced the the gossip needed to lighten a desperate situation in the vessels small community ... and the meals improved too.

The South Tasman Rise is storm riddled. The storm fronts start in the Antarctic Ocean, south of Heard Island and have over a thousand sea miles to gather a head of steam without any land modification. The fronts produce giant rollers that beget rogue waves and when the swells hit the South Tasman Rise, they

---

[1]Waid-H: What am I doing here?

interact with the sub-tropical air mass. The *convergent zone* is the drain hole for the continents high-pressure air mass.

There are spectacular electric storms at the STR Roughy grounds. The storms don't arrive flashing and rumbling from a far horizon. Instead, they erupt above you, with a strobe-like flash and milliseconds later by a thunder-boom which rattles every loose fitting on the boat. It's like experiencing a blitzkrieg and it embeds awe, before fear sets in. It could be a coincidence but many fish spawns [around the world] start after powerful electrical storms.

The *Monica* was built to handle rotten weather and as long as its bow had a thin quarter to the oncoming sea, it handled the power of the Southern Ocean well. Fishing was suspended only when the engine couldn't produce headway with the nets out.

Just when the crew's mood was starting to get shitty again, our heavy steel mast-top came down, severed from its crossbar platform on a line of failed bolts.

The autopilot failed to keep the vessel on its set course and the side-on seas shifted the mast top over the roof with horrendous steel-on-steel graunching noises. These were followed by the crashing noises of impedance as the mast top hit the combing. The wire-stays held the severed steel acting like a tether and making sure it remained [noisily] on the roof.

Hand steering the vessel downwind stopped the worst of the noise and provided a stable ship to repair the wreckage. The uppermost fitting on the mast had been a GPS receiving unit and although we had two units, the second unit was wiped out when the mast top had collapsed.

We had other satellite feeds giving read outs of our position and heading but these weren't integrated with the autopilot and it making it impossible to fish with accuracy. We set a course to Hobart for repairs. Sometimes a sea-life takes you to some nice ports and Hobart is one of those. Approaching from the river, Hobart had charm without a building crane in sight.

Alasker & the Tiger ₀₀₀₀

Marty Alasker was keen to visit the museum and see what a stuffed Tasmanian tiger looked like [real size]. The oddity of the Tasmanian tiger intrigued him. He knew the facts. He knew how they could open their jaws wider than any other mammal. He knew they were a *carnivorous* marsupial with a pouch that opens to the rear.

"Their extinction happened in a zoo," and he went on with the sort of fact bombs he loved dropping when given a half chance, and more so when he was excited.

A one and tuppeny stamp showing Tasmanian tiger

As soon as we tied up, Marty disembarked [dressed in best], yelling over his shoulder, "Waterfront museums are the only good thing about fishing."

He loved being first man off any boat he worked on and he loved a mission in a new city. The crew, who just wanted to hit the pubs, sat waiting in the quiet of his absence for their turn in the shower.

Less than an hour later, he was back reporting the museum didn't have a Tasmanian tiger, in fact, the museum didn't have a Tasmanian devil.

He wailed, "There was a bit of tassie tiger film-footage and the film looked like it had been to the brink of extinction." He wailed on about the museum being full of coins that were engraved with country names from all around the world, display box after display box filled with coins that were minted by the convicts. He moaned loudly, "It's just overly spiteful getting transported convicts to mint money".

When we left Hobart, our bosses had a new fishing plan which involved the seamounts to the south of the roughy feature. These seamounts had populations of small Black Dory and medium-sized Smooth Dory. The plan was to catch smoothies and locate some blacks of marketable size while keeping an eye on the roughy feature, [when all else fails try a triple-juggling manoeuvre].

Catching dories, with article 7 enforced, meant a pitiful pay because the small fish were un-marketable. The Ministry had taken over the responsibilities of the fisherman and the crew weren't being paid fairly. The other vessels were Australian licensed and they didn't have to keep anything they couldn't unload for a sale.

The situation wasn't helped when Salpa marks starting to appear on the grounds. In places, the Salpa clusters were a hundred metres high. Salpas are jelly creatures that look like exotic condoms when they come to the ocean surface.

The first sighting of a Salpa, your mind goes '*condom*' and if it doesn't you would be considered a bit odd. No condom manufacturer could dream up a Salpa shape or its pleasant iridescence. They are one of nature's oddities. However, day old Salpa stuck in the nets start to smell like discarded condoms!

There was lively debate about the salps regarding article 7. Were they a jelly? Were they a fish?

"They eat their own brains out and become barnacles." Marty had interrupted a meeting with a flash fact for the unenlightened.

The debate only ended when the Salpa were declared to be cellulose [plant material] and we were allowed to discard them.

A bit about Salpas ₒ ₒ ₒ ₒ

A single Salpa is an oozooid [what a word] and a chain of salps is called a blastozooid. Salpas are colonial and they can self-clone by throwing a bud. They are hermaphrodites for self-procreation [no sex changes necessary]. A Salpa has a million times more vanadium in its blood than the marine soup they live in. A big swarm of salps, reported off California, was thousands of square miles in size.

Salpas migrate to the surface on a daily basis and are a good fishing indicator. They can grow in size by 10% an hour. Salpas are the most important carbon sink in the ocean [and probably the planet] and they are responsible for keeping krill under control.

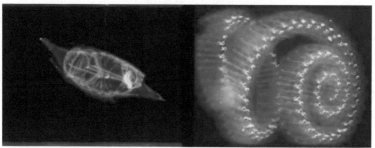

A single Salpa [left] ....and a chain of Salps [right]

Salpas have a habit of forming large clusters on the side of deep rocks. When clustered up, they look like fish marks [on a sounder]. At the STR that year, their massive presence caused frustration.

Unlike fish, the Salpa signal marks never change shape but often their sounder trace can appear like fish. We caught our share of salps before we left the STR.

We all wanted to scarper from the STR. On the boat it had become known as the '*straightjacket rise*'. Our management [with all the good ideas], didn't pursue lost causes and they were quick to change their minds about our 'triple-juggle' fishing act. We refuelled and restocked our stores on another visit to Hobart. The refuel allowed us to go fishing at the Lord Howe Rise.

We felt like we could get a load at the *Howe Foul* and we were bullish about it. Seven tonnes of Roughy a tonne of decaying article 7 bycatch in the freezers can do that to you. We weren't permitted to unload at Hobart but we left with fresh food, high blood booze levels and only one arrest [disorderly behaviour].

We were off to the Lord Howe Rise and the positive mood escalated as the straightjacket feeling eased. You trusted your luck on Lord Howe trips. The rise is a weather beaten place in the middle of the Tasman Sea and a dangerous area to hunt.

We headed to the middle of '*the foul*', to an area where the fish had first been worked outside New Zealand waters a decade before. It was called the Howe Foul by the early fisherman and it was a great description for the area, which is like fifty-thousand hectares of the most rugged mountain country.

We had an old disk of the area – the disk had once been the subject of an unsuccessful court case. One thing we could be sure of was any feature we found that wasn't on the disk, was new and un-harvested.

The disk was the *witch doctor's* work and the marks had pinpoint accuracy. Alas the Howe Foul only produced more Salpa. The creatures were spread over the whole of Tasman Sea roughy grounds.

The small catch returns from the Tasman and Lord Howe Rises allowed the owners to provision the vessel for a Louisville trip. We would be saved the financial ruin of a bad season by the Louisville Ridge. Skipper Heals had been bullish about it, he told me he'd show me a thing or two [and I believed him]. Once more optimism was rampant.

Louisville Ridge - June [2000] ○ ○ ○ ○

We arrived at the thirty-seven seamount at the north-end of the Louisville Ridge in early June. Skipper Heals had ran over a pimple-sized rock-pile [C] at the south-end of the feature the year before on his first pass across the grounds. Previous fishing effort had concentrated at the other end of the seamount [A] ten nautical miles away.

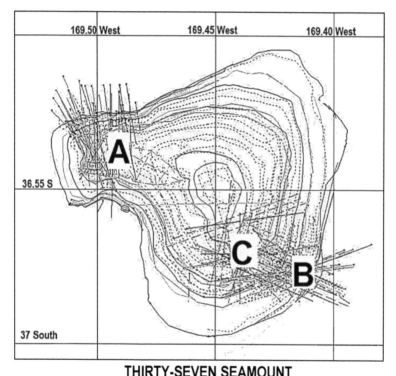

THIRTY-SEVEN SEAMOUNT
Progressive contours and trawl tows.
A]. Original fish: B]. Bank Fish: C]. *The Pimple 935metres*

Heals had lucked the new discovery, the year before, but the fish had dissipated before he could get a good harvest. He was hoping the fish would re-appear in year 2000 at the same place and he was in luck again. We started catching spawning fish

113

immediately and we had thirty tonnes of product in the hold after three days. A good catch was looking realistic because the fish were regularly turning up for two hours in the early evening. Regular catches suit a factory trawler.

We had more good luck when we found fish marks over the side-edge [B] they were spunked-up males, and they turned up at dawn, and the new discovery put the factory into maximum processing mode.

It was no surprise when Salpa marks started to appear although we were sure the marks we were trawling were fish doubts clouded every trawl as they say `fishing is a thing that makes confidence its first victim`.

We were catching salps but we were landing good bags of Roughy. It came to a halt when, without warning, the vessel's exhaust emitted a plume of black smoke and started making the noises that suggest imperfect combustion.

In the wheelhouse, the quiet accompanying the high expectation of another good trawl was replaced with swearing. The profanities were a backbeat to the exhaust backfiring. The vessel slowed and the occasional red flame ignited at the exhaust flue-mouth before the main engines shut down automatically.

The trawl winches and fish factory were powered by their own auxiliary engine enabling the gear to be retrieved and the fish factory to process the fifteen tonne of Roughy catch.

The Chief Engineer for the trip [Mick] reported the turbocharger was 'pakaru gonski, stuffed and kaput'. He was wearing his big-job overalls and he was looking deadly serious. We lay too and Mick blanked off the turbo using parts stowed in purpose-built racks since the vessels launch and never used.

We limped home through a couple of storms so slowly Marty

Alasker[1] reckoned jellyfish were passing us. Sometimes we barely progressed. It took us over a week to complete a trip that normally took two days. The fish at `thirty seven` would have to wait another year

Louisville Ridge - 2000

After the turbo repairs were completed, we headed to the bottom of the Louisville Ridge to finish the Roughy season. At the 45°s seamount, we got a load and a pay. Forty-five was classic rollover fishing and the fish were using a small window of opportunity to spawn. We joined in with the zeal of tax collectors but it was no surprise when Salpa marks started to appear.

It made us wonder why these creatures had decided to take over the Southern Ocean. We had encountered them over almost three thousand nautical miles and it was a safe bet they were over the whole of the `roaring forties latitudes`. The year 2000 was Salpa year, perhaps massive krill numbers were feeding their expansion or was it the excess carbon dioxide in the air mass?

It had been a long season. The boat was looking tired, after seven months at sea. When maintenance should have been done we were busy dealing with the three major breakdowns. The NZ flag of registry which had been hoisted from the aft flagpole, before the season began, was now a tattered remnant.

---

[1] This would be Marty Alasker's last trawl trip. According to the latest rumour, he is now living in outback Australia.

8...Plunder at the Ridge

Auckland - March [2001] ₒₒₒₒ

We fished the vessel *Seamount Explorer* II and worked out of the downtown Auckland wharves in 2001. The *Seamount* was owned by the Barbarich family and their company had started the worldwide trade in Orange Roughy.

The boat was a forty-four metre; 1620kW long-range fresh-fish boat and it already had success at the Louisville Ridge. We would be working both sides of the EEZ line and spend time working the Bay Of Plenty seamounts.

My electronic database of the features and fishing tows at the Louisville Ridge got me the job, the rumours I knew the whereabouts of fish at the thirty-seven seamount helped. Wizza [Johnston] was the skipper and he was busy South Islandizing the crew when I arrived there. The South Islanders were excited when they arrived; they told stories about airport security confiscating their beloved deck knives and being stung by the taxi operators.

Some of the new arrivals were having their first big-city experience and they had new stories on a daily basis – encounters with con-artists and trawling transvestites can do that to you. After three days in port, the nightlife started to tell. Cell phones were getting lost quicker than new ring-tones were being installed and insurance claims were filling in the crews' slack time while we waited to sail.

Wizza had employed the South Islanders because he knew them and he knew they had the skills he needed to bring big bags of fish on-board. They were all good on a surge drum [with wire or rope] and they had doctorates [uncertificated] in shovelling ice and throwing fish.

The South Islanders had a sense of community; they had jump-to attitudes, no-pain barriers, and teamwork. They had the things needed for a season at the Louisville Ridge on an iceboat - but they were the things that needled the northerners. That year parochial provocation was rampart at the downtown wharfs, the Aucklanders were having fun at the South Islanders expense, and the *mainlanders* took it well.

"The further north you go; the better the pay – *it's a fact!*" the witchdoctor, [a South Islander] had said while we were docked in Lyttleton in 1994 and he was right, and the North Island crews should thank the Auckland Fishing Guild [and diamond smile McKinnon]. Wizza thought it was a situation of the northerners, not knowing how good they had it.

In Auckland, deckys earn as much as a forty-foot skipper down in the South Island. On the other-hand, around the Auckland Wharfs 2001 [pre-curtain-raising Americas Cup], a custard square cost you as much as a breakfast and coffee on the other side of Cook Strait [as long as you didn't buy it on the ferry].

Our crew finished a mixture of four North Island, five South Island and an honorary South Islander from Hull [Hindsey]. Hindsey had come to New Zealand in the early days of the fishing expansion and he'd kept nets for the best.

North or South Islander the crew had multi-social problems, [bordering on the near-side of normal]. The casino and tattoo parlours were open all night, the dance parties went past breakfast and some of them weren't getting enough sleep in nightlife paradise but none of them got arrested.

Most of the crew lived to excess and excused it with, "You're only young once." I was taunted for being old, I loved being old, I'd earned every grey hair in my beard and it meant the crew, with a teen angst which would see them well into middle age, didn't see free to share things with me. Their teasing sort of made me jealous until memories of good catches came into focus. Good catches would mean the `only young-once` deck-crew would spend twenty-four hours immersed in ice, throwing thousands of fish two at a time and the aftermath of the hard work was a welter of wet socks and utter exhaustion.

Church Club - May [2001] ○ ○ ○ ○

The *Seamount* had been busy fishing *inside* the line [200-mile EEZ] and in May, I got a trip off before the Louisville Orange Roughy season began. Roughy prices were on the rise and the weather was in a westerly pattern. You could sense a good season at `The Ridge`.

One night, [at the Church Club], my confidence about a good catch and my imagination, were both big. I was wearing my new 'braggadocio' T-shirt and my chest was inflated with optimism. When anyone asked me how the fishing was going I raved on about the season ahead and I raved on about how big weather systems starting the prawn swarming and the plankton performing, I raved on about massive up-wellings and the half knot abysmal sea current. I tried to explain it clearly but I digressed a few times [often] and I totally bamboozled the listeners to the point of bewilderment.

Flash [McBride] was there and he was calling out loud, "All roughy fishermen are plunderers." I hoped it was a fitting name-call but the fish were still to be caught and I knew the plunder days at the Louisville Ridge were gone.

At the time, accident insurance levies had put the self-employed fisherman of New Zealand into financial crisis by charging them for accidents they never had, it was called *catch up* and it had you praying for a good season

I was in a position to accept anything described as plunder, [even plunder with a very small p]. I thought of the Louisville Ridge's 37°s seamount, and the fish marks over its bank that were left untouched when the *Santa Monica* blew its turbo. We had been trying to harvest the seamount for three years yet one of the great fish commentators was in the parliamentary Hansard records saying...

"New Zealanders were amongst the worst of the words fishing people. An example is the way the Orange Roughy fisheries on the Louisville Ridge have been systematically plundered and virtually destroyed almost entirely by New Zealand fishers. They have gone from one undersea mountain to another systematically raping and pillaging those natural resources".

Going from one seamount to another was slightly over the top. The fish started spawning in the high latitudes and spawning times were progressively later in the south. We had been chasing a spawn school harvest at the 37° seamount for three years and it was 3-0 nil to the fish and presumably a lot of fertilized eggs had incubated in that time. The bit about raping and pillaging looked good on paper but I had plunder on my mind...

I could hear the noises of another big bag of fish coming on board,

I could hear the swaged twenty-eight-mil wire humming as it tightened into the lay and stretched close to breaking point,

I could hear the thudding of the loaded wire as it settled with a crunch into the vacant grooves on the winch drums,

...I could hear the guide-on gear clunking and tapping on the drive sprockets,

...and the hydraulics relieving noisily in the background, sounding sometimes like a strangled hose and sometimes like a rocket at take-off.

I could imagine the warps, painted every fifty metres, slow wrapping on a slowly revolving drum. I could picture the small gains being made getting the huge catch aboard.

I day dreamed the things associated with the plunder...

Skipper yelling – the deck boss perplexed - the double snatch blocks twisting-up and the cook wanting to make a phone call.`
... We were off to plunder the Ridge.

The Vessel & the Fishing Gear ₀ ₀ ₀ ₀

Seamount Explorer II : GT 671 LOA 44m [Previously FV Europa].

The *Seamount Explorer* II was German design and build. It was a well-maintained modern trawler in 2001 and it had features that weren't on older trawlers. It was the days when every trawler arriving in the country was also an example of trawler innovation and electronic development.

The sounder on the *Seamount* was computer driven with sophisticated fine-tuning features. It`s memory was capable of displaying grounds by historic time or geographical position from years before and the historic replays were a useful tool when studying fish-marks or bottom topography.

The *Seamount* had two net monitor displays which was a handy advance for pinnacle fishing. The two-monitor set up meant there was less to do when the fisherman was busy watching headline height and boat speed at the business end of the tow. Using one monitor and switching views caused display time lags, at the crossover and at times, it created some confused situations. With the two-monitor set up, the fisherman could relax a little and watch headline height and the depth as the net progressed down the pinnacle

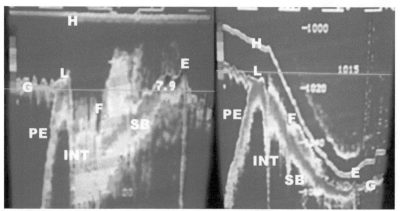

Look down Picture　　　　**True Motion monitor Picture**

L ~ Net landing on pinnacle　F~ Fish under headline
H ~ Net headline　　　　　　 PE ~ Edge of Pinnacle
E ~ Net lifting off sea bed　　 G ~ Net ground gear
INT ~ Interference　　　　　　SB ~ Sea bed
　　* Look down monitor shows headline height at 7.9 metres
　　* True Motion monitor shows net landing at 1015 metres and the
　　　　cursor line can be moved to obtain net depth
　　*Signal interference [INT] after net landing [L] is caused by the net
　　　　slowing and the headline/monitor lifting.
　　*Lines above headline [H] are minute time marks [5 minute trawl]

The *Seamount* had a purpose-built net roller, other trawlers had net rollers that had been built at the local engineering shops and foundries, but this roller was a recessed design-feature, with its controls in the wheelhouse.

121

The controls, for everything you might need, were micro-control and laid out each side of a seated operations area overlooking the deck. The winch-drivers station had windows all around including the floor [like a tail-gunners-bubble] and its seat was hydraulically dampened with first-class comfort.

When I first sat in the winch-drivers' seat, memories from a decade before, on the trawler Cook Canyon started flooding back ...

...when we stood on a slippery, wobbly, sheet of under-sized ply, two decks up, in a roaring Cook Strait gale and shoulder charged the net onto the roller-drum while a smiling Smithy got drenched on the lever control.

The Seamounts deck machinery was automated: the yo-yo [for pulling the net off the deck], paravane [for receiving the signals from the net monitor], and the wave-gate were controlled from the wheelhouse. Steering and pitch controls could be operated from the winch drivers station.

The wave gate moved out of the deck vertically from a recess near the stern ramp and it had a roller on its top edge saving wire wear when the gear was being shot or retrieved. The gate was capable of lifting the bridle or sweep wires to make repairs or changes, an easy task. It was the sort of feature every big-trawler deckhand had dreamed about, and wondered why, the naval architects hadn't added the so obvious design component.

About Fishing Techniques &Roughy ○ ○ ○ ○

The art of Roughy fishing is to use the gear [net and sweeps] to herd the fish down underwater slopes until the decrease in temperatures and oxygen supply makes them tire and turn towards the net-mouth.

Normally when you have a good catch there are a few *"sticker-fish"* stuck in the wings. The stickers catch because of pressure differentials or the net isn't square and they get snagged around broken meshes and loose mesh. If one side of the net is out of shape [at its wings] relative to the trawl, it has a bunt billowing out to the side and fish will lodge in it.

"One sticker; one tonne, two stickers two tonne," Larry [from Stewart Island] used to say with unerring accuracy. He was talking tons of catch for every observed sticker in the wings. The wings are the first part of the net to come on board and stickers are first indication of a catch.

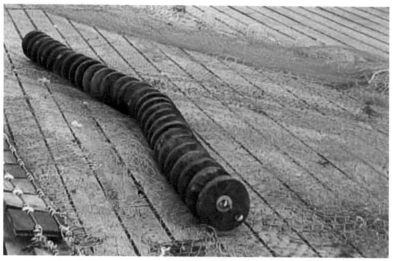

A section of rock-hopper ground-gear [G].

The *Seamount Explorers* trawl gear was heavy. The *ground gear* was a version of rock hopper and it had rubber discs close to a metre in diameter. The discs were doubled-up, side by side [probably a Bray brainwave], with heavy chain threaded through them to attach the net [and add weight]. All the chain connections were protected by solid rubber sleeves.

On the *Seamount* Explorer, there were *sticker fish* caught head first between the double rubber-discs and they required a strong, almost Herculean tug, to extricate them. We called the trapped fish *road kill* and they got you wondering about the Roughy's natural instinct to go under a net.

Louisville Ridge, May [2001] ○ ○ ○ ○

The Louisville Roughy spawn happens at the same time [day/month] every year. The times are different for the various seamounts but they are consistent. It is as though the Orange Roughy have a Julian calendar.

Major spawn areas are associated with large salients and deep canyons and the canyons reach to the abysmal sea five-thousand metres below the ocean surface. At the shallow end of these canyons, the fishable spawn spots are in gullies close to large outcrop rocks or fissures. The spawn activity takes advantage of the upwellings and counter currents. There is usually an area of ooze or some other soft substrate nearby. The scoria or ooze contains shrimp and shellfish. The shrimp burrow into the soft bottom and breathe through their feelers, while they are shedding their shells and vulnerable to predators.

I have a theory that, at spawn time of the year, the currents triggered by upwellings start the winter prawn shell-shed. Migratory Orange Roughy males move with the currents from the holding grounds. When the resident Roughy females start feeding on the prawns, the mixture of mud and pheromones attracts the males to the area for egg fertilization. Females lost during spawning are replaced by males, who then change sex. We have caught fish with organs of both sexes

In late May, we were off to the Louisville Ridge with Clive [Bray] as skipper. We timed our departure for the Ridge and the timing would have us arriving at the *Thirty-seven* seamount at spawn time. We expected to plunder the fish we left behind when the *Santa Monica* had blown its turbo and we thought they would be relatively easy to find a year later.

124

We were a fifty miles from the Ridge when a message came through on the Immarsat-C fax system from Clive's father and the message changed the trip forever. Colin [Clive's father] had skimmed down the Ridge looking for early pickings and got as far as the seamount at 38°30 south where he 'shot a mark' but had come fast and lost most of his fishing gear.

In the fishing industry, everyone assists fellow fishermen with troubles; it is the rule with trawler-men and definitely with a family concern. Hindsey [the bosun from Hull] was ordered to start putting together a set of gear we could pass over to Colin's boat [Waipori]. A new course was set to the seamount at 38°30 south and it was two hundred miles below our target destination.

Most boats carry at least a set and a half of spare gear; such is the nature of the far ocean fishing game. However the father and son team had lost net parts that weren't normally carried as spares [on the smaller trawlers] so they couldn't make up another rig.

The rest of our trip was a story of slim pickings and grumpiness. All the boats that went to the Ridge, including the two that secured a good catch at the 37° seamount were reporting small spawn aggregations with large female fish. The female-catch produced oversize fillets and the finished product was bigger than the 4 to 6oz[1] market preference. The fish were producing a 20oz fillet which had to be cut. When an expensive product is being sold, cut fillets don't have a good plate presence.

It was the year with no snow on Ruapehu, my dreams of plunder had deflated, [and the Australian company that brought the North Island ski-fields were heading broke because of the no snow show].

---

[1] Export fish is traded in $US and weights (5oz = 112 g, 20oz. = 569g).

Inside the Line - [2001] ○ ○ ○ ○

After the Louisville season, we started fishing the deep seamounts off the West Coast of the North Island. We were Roughy fishing for the North American fresh fish market and the fishing was slow. Roughy were fetching premium prices, but the fishing trips incurred time restrictions because the product had to be landed at San Diego in a super-fresh state. The short trips meant small catches and small pays.

In September, we caught a big catch on the first night out. It was big enough to pay the bills, with money left over for wastage, and shrinkage. We headed into port on a happy boat. In the early dawn hours, I was on watch as we passed by the Cavallis north of Auckland. Jim [The Sniff] rang earlier than was usual for him. He was a punctual ship's husband who gathered reports from the skippers before the city came to life.

"Did you hear the news?" he asked.

"Yes," I'd answered, "Canterbury 22 Auckland 6"

"No," he said, "The world news."

"I've been playing CDs and listening to songs from the lost seaway," I'd replied, "I always listen to them when we have a good trip. How are the fish prices?"

"Terrorists have destroyed the Twin Towers in New York. They've flown planes into them," He was excited. "It's on the TV live."

I told him we were passing the Cavallis and there was no television reception in the area.

"All the airports in the States are closed and we can't send any fish there so don't hurry into port."

You couldn't help thinking about the vagaries of the fresh fish market.

9...Sapun Gora

Taranaki - May [2002] o o o o

Just past Hangi Tapu on a trip to Wheramoamoa, my cell phone started on a beeping shutdown and the car radio went through a static death. I had a poetry moment. All hunts should begin with a verse or two. The bad verse blossomed in my mind [involuntarily – I tell you] as I drove towards the Piko Valley, north of New Plymouth

> *At 'Broken Gate Farm'*
> *Up 'Stock on the Road'*
> *There's a blind black cow*
> *chewing cud in the fog -*
> *while a very muddy puddle*
> *is lapped at...*
> *by a pup and a dog*

> *It's a narrow siding valley*
> *sunless in winter*
> *The place Roughy would live*
> *...If it was underwater*

> *And the rushes grow high*
> *as a bobby calf's eye*
> *and in some places...*
> *a-hellava-lot bigger.*

There was a tin bus shelter [no graffiti or bullet holes] and a new concrete power pole, with a new stock sign. Everything matched where I had been told to turn off. The road had no name-post but there were signs, **School Bus Turns, Windy Road next 50kms, No Exit,** and **Stock**.

I turned off the tar seal onto a clay-cut road with a good cover of river gravel. But after a kilometre, the road changed to a light cover of crusher-run and the sound of the chipped-rock hitting the cars` floor-pan suggested armour-piercing bullets. The poetry soothed recovered memories of bad breakdowns on back-block country roads, while the roading-rock was stoning the car to death.

The rutted road with no name had end-to-end hairpin bends and deep unavoidable potholes and there were plenty of *Stock on the road* signs. On the low side of the road, there were tractor skid-tracks in the mud, and puddles, leading to flattened gates. I thundered on in the drizzle, the mist, and the rain at 30 k/hour *'with an ear-to-ear grin and a cacophony of rattling'*. Poetry with potency, those moments don't happen often. I couldn't help thinking deep-seated worries and insecurities were surfacing.

Stu had told me he lived at the end of the road. The road arced around the bluffs beside a small roily river. The road crossed streams and washouts and in the gorges there were evidential flood heights showing high on the walls. Everywhere was the evidence of slips and repairs. Where there were riverside flats, beside the road, they were overgrown with rushes. On the roads high side there were occasionally glimpses of grazed pasture grass beneath a canopy of mature Manuka and the ridge spurs were covered in pig fern and Pungas with the occasional Mamuku cutting the skyline.

It was back blocks country [*out the back of remote*], where you could get lost, without effort, but Stu had said, "There are no side roads. Stop at the first woolshed on the left. You'll see the house from there," then he added "Mind the black cow on the road - it's blind, don't worry about the dogs, they don't bite." Definitive directions, I thought, '*bring on the big black blind cow*'.

Stu had an idyllic lifestyle [for the hen-pecked]. He had a mix of backcountry farming and far-ocean trawlers. He had confided in me, on a previous fishing trip, that he thought women would have liked his backcountry lifestyle, but he'd been wrong. He had been trying to find the 'ideal' backcountry woman for a long time. He had charm but it hadn't helped in his search for the lady of Broken Gate farm.

When the woolshed loomed out of the fog, the black cow leapt from the road showing a swinging tail and little evidence of blindness. Stu dogs welcomed me at the gate with wet paws and puddle mouths.

Stu and I were due to fish a large Ukrainian vessel leaving for the Louisville Ridge from Lyttelton but our sailing date was delayed when the Ukraine Government was slow to sign an International Agreement. The signing of the agreement would permit us to fish from New Zealand. Without the agreement, we would have to work out of a Pacific Island port.

Waiting for boats was something both of us could handle and we'd both done it many times. Waiting for an international agreement to be signed, was new.

'*There's always work on the farm,*' so we chipped, cut and mowed rushes while we waited. It was premium rushy country. Ditches and farm roads had disappeared under their spines.

When the agreement was ratified we travelled south in Stu's farm truck. The truck had a tarp over a tray-load of things Stu thought he might need for the trip. He'd been secretive about his supplies but an inner-sprung mattress was hard to hide and it hinted that comfort was a factor. I expected discomfort, from a maritime point of view it was hard to imagine anything more basic than a Soviet trawler.

On the way south, we were ogling the girls as we passed through the populated areas. It was obvious we had both been in the backblocks too long [and the fact we were off to sea didn't help]. Our rubbernecking was going to cause an accident, so we set up a watch system whereby we took turns at driving on a town-by-town rotation in an effort to stay safe. Stu, being the skipper, set up the roster and as usual when skippers set up watches - it is always unfair.

By the time we got to Plimmerton, where Glover had seen '*Penguins at play and an albatross at Karehana Bay*', the girl watching was over and Stu was eyeing the city petrol prices, which are like milestones to a fisherman from Wheramoamoa.

Surge - Catch Report June [2002] ○ ○ ○ ○

We waited overnight to catch the inter-island ferry. I rang Surge. to tell him I was back in cell phone range for a day or two before I was off on another roughy hunt and to plan a conger session on my return. He reported he'd caught enough Congers to get us a good catch history.

He thought small freights could produce adequate returns if we had good logistics. It was a concern needing thought. I pictured coffee, percolating to a mud-like mixture, on Surge's wood-range. Surge did all his thinking drinking unhealthy amounts of strong coffee. He confided the mail blitzkrieg he had been experiencing had died down. The injured deckhands were off ACC and his nephew [Tai] had gone plucking opossums for a living at the Coromandel. The malformed conger-damaged thumb was good for the job.

Surge went on, at length, about why he had changed the tail-fins on the Conger catchers. He is always meticulously longwinded when describing minor-engineering marvels and worse when he is having a justification moment. Surge delivers intricate descriptions of the mechanics and brain processes involved [while mentioning all the people he has discussed it with and their responses]. This in turn digresses to news of those people and what they have been doing updates. He went on too long and he said '*um*' too many times. Worse still, I was paying for the phone call! I was off to sea and was about to partake of the last party, so I cut him off, even though I knew I would feel guilty about doing it.

Stu and I spent the night in Wellington and we played *hicks in the city* as grownup country boys do. We had our photos taken at the *Blue Note* with our arms around 'new-found' friends of dubious gender. At a strip club across the road, we brought large glossy pics of ourselves [centre photo] with the stars. We competed for lap dancers and Stu said it was always better when Yeti wasn't there[1]. Then we headed to the early morning

---

[1] A Yeti is bigger than a horse and Yeti the decky hogged the lap dancers if he was there.

bars to wait for the ferry departure. It was a night of no real consequence, but would be fuel for conversation during the fishing trip. The photos were evidence of an over-indulgence we hoped to repeat.

After the ferry crossing to Picton, we drove south being very frugal [*pacing the pies*] and talked fishing. Maxed out credit cards [and a pocket full of worthless *showgirl dollars*] had caused the conversation change. We were on a hunt and someone had taken a risk and put up a boat, a crew, and a quarter million dollars [U.S] for fuel. We offered high hopes, the position of last year's fish and a good database of the Louisville Ridge to help with success.

Lyttelton - [2002] ○ ○ ○ ○

Soviet bloc fishing vessels were docked at the major ports in New Zealand in 2002. They had a fascination factor and I always dreamed of working one of them. When the sombre-coloured Soviet trawlers are sitting against the wharf, they look like they are in hibernation and the attitudes of the crew suggests a *Bleak Ship* situation. However, when we arrived at the Lyttelton wharves, the *Sapun Gora* was bustling with activity and some of the crew were smiling.

We were greeted by the ship's agent who had a joint venture arrangement with a Christchurch company [United Fisheries]. He was cheerful but he left straight after introducing himself and we didn't see him again until after the trip

The *Sapun Gora* didn't have any trawl-wire on the winch drums. Checking wire is compulsive for roughy fisherman and "What's the wire like?" is the standard industry question whenever trawlers are discussed.

It is a big job to put two-and-a-half thousand metres of wire on each drum while painting it every fifty metres with identifying marks [even if it is quick drying paint]. The wire has to be spooled onto the drums equally and tightly so it can be deployed evenly without overriding.

SAPUN GORA..2554 GT . LOA 82m

The net-master [Mishka] said the wire would be done by the morning and he added, "Measured and marked." He was reassuring about his declaration so we offered to take him to lunch. When we asked what type of food he liked, he answered with a surety, "Potatoes."

We were confused but we took him to a local buffet where potatoes were boiled, roasted, mashed, chipped, wedged, [and salad`ed]. He was a man of his word, potatoes were his thing, and he dined on spuds for almost an hour while we discussed our net plans [and spuds]. Mishka knew his potatoes [and nets], he told us that Ukrainians were the biggest potato eaters in the world and they had been eating them since the Spanish brought them back from Peru. I recounted a school history lesson, [which was worth a point or two in a minor exam], that we were taught the British [Sir Walter Raleigh] were the first to bring potatoes from America. Mishka said, 'maybe' but the

Spanish took them to America long before the British got there. I made a remark about Irelands potato famine but I was rebuked with the details of the 'Holodomor' a spud holocaust. He liked New Zealand potatoes and commented that it was good to have so many tasty varieties. Mishka wanted us to know that on the vessel, the potato peelings were 'strictly supervised' because the crew used them to brew vodka.

Mishka didn't come back to the boat with us and he said we would have to discuss our wire set-ups [bridle and sweeps] with the deck bosses.

When we returned to the vessel, we were confronted with the language difficulties we would have on the trip. A deck hand with a manner of minor importance [his comrades in close company] asked us questions about wire configuration, and paint markings. The questions needed a great deal of interpretation to decipher and answer. We had established one, two, three was *adyn, divois, tree* but little else before the Sapun Gora`s interpreter-mate [good English] arrived, he apologised and quickly resolved the problems before leading us on a tour of the boat. The interpreter was twentyish and impish and proudly revealed he was from a large family of seafarers who had been sea going for `*many-many*` generations.

The deck crews were big men and the word `*bears*` sprung to mind without prompting [and somehow the word 'eunuch' made an indelible mark on my brain]. As we left the deck, the deckies were using derricks to move huge stacks of mid-water nets. It's always a good sight, seeing large loads shifted with double-derrick teamwork. The pivoted-arms were swinging as if to handshake and a bosun was conducting their movement wit lazy hand signals.

Mid-water fishing is the Ukrainian forte. Some of their nets have twenty bridles and forty metres of headline height. They are the sort of nets that could contain a building the size of a fish factory.

The *Sapun Gora* had a big wheelhouse with full width windows that gave a hunter's platform view. On the portside of the bridge deck, was a large four-person couch. The interpreter explained this would be our fishing station when the electronics were set in place. The thought of working from a couch of such magnitude, even if it was shabby, was novel. Stu [who had worked the boat before] hadn't mentioned a couch and he certainly hadn't mentioned a five-seater couch at the centre of the operations.

I couldn't resist giving the faded seat on the couch a flat palm slap to feel the comfort level. The impulse had a bad result - it created a plume eruption of dust [almost mushroom-shaped] and from the corner of my eye, I noticed an officer with a worried brow, sloping off to the furthermost corner of the wheelhouse. The plume was probably asbestos-dust which had collected in the aged upholstery. All the trawlers [and warships] from the fifties had asbestos insulation falling out of the bulkheads.

It was obvious the fallout worried the bridge crew, but we were all in the 'same boat' when it came to dealing with it. One option was ignoring it to the point of denial and not patting the couch, but the problem was solved when a sub-protégé, [looking embarrassed], appeared with a plastic cover-all and his delivery made everyone seem at ease.

The wheelhouse scullery was a cockroach feeding ground and the cockroaches seemed to salute [with their feelers] while they patrolled the area. Sea folk have enough stories to clog up a small IT network about ships and roaches. On this vessel, the roaches reached an ugly size and walked around like miniature dinosaurs. The Ukrainians ignored the roaches and put lids on their cups to save any annoyance. Stu said the cockroaches were worse on his last trip and he was probably being truthful.

We had brought our own coffee. Stu said it could be used as a bribe for civil behaviour and that the Soviets only used their own coffee on special occasions.

Our guide, using a key from a wear-polished ring, opened a locked wall-box below the water jug and lidded cups. The lock looked antique and a work of art. The keys on the ring were impressive, even their jingling noise was impressive. The key ring was brass with a craftsman's clasp and the keys were different, in shape and colour. Those keys could very well have been the type that kept the Cold War cold.

Our cheerful guide opened the door-lock with a small key that had gone golden with use. The cabinet contained a kilo-pack of sugar and three tins of condensed milk. He raised his brow and his pixie-like-face suggested forlornness. He picked up a can of condensed milk and said with a knowing smile "Two hours of hubble-bubble." and then he did an impression of a man in a stupor with his eyes rolling counter clockwise.

He picked up the sugar and repeated the hubble-bubble bit, but this time when he did the eye rolling, he added reverberating lips and raspberry noises. Our obvious amusement encouraged him to do an encore and then he said,

"They make alcohol." You could gather `they` were everyone but him. From then on, I amused myself with a game of `spot the distiller` until it dawned on me, that all the crew and officers [except one] were probably moon-shiners.

The keeper of the keys took our coffee and asked if we would need sugar. He stored our supplies, and locked the cabinet, then hung the keys on his belt with a flourish that sent a peal of brassy-noise into the airwaves.

Brass is used on vessels where a metal fixture is subject to salt water or salt-spray. On this vessel, there was polished brass everywhere. Door handles, rubbing strips, knobs, guardrails, label plates, and floor hatch pulls shone from its presence.

You could imagine the *Sapun Gora*, had a brass cleaning detachment whose elbows and shoulders were strong, who had a dedication to annihilate any wisp of verdigris or film of oxidation.

Brass is expensive and not something that ship owners care

to buy, [and a few have been known to baulk at buying brass washers or screws]. It was obvious they didn't skimp on brass in the Soviets. The brass stood out in a wheelhouse that was grey with shades of grey and it seemed a suitable colour scheme; if you were having a Cold War.

Many of the crew were overly dressed in well-known designer labelled clothing, the showy garments were the products of Ukrainian sweatshops. The crew traded the 'label' garments [seconds and rejects], which allowed them to survive on the meagre wages they earned. A Ukrainian fisherman's typical tour of duty is eleven months away from home and the pay equates to eight thousand dollars US. Their airfare [four thousand] is deducted, but they don't pay tax.

Our guide said, "They can buy a new Lada car with one year's pay. Lada is still the best vehicle for exhaust suicides," the keeper of the keys joked, "This is the only time, when a Lada is faster."

The officer's dining mess was on an upper level with a dumb waiter connecting it to the galley. It was smallish by comparison to the size of the vessel, but it had silver cutlery and starched linen tablecloths. The embroidered napkins were folded like fans and reminiscent of colonial splendour.

I'm a greasy-spoon-cafe sort of a guy who was brought up eating from boarding-school troughs. I have an aversion to eating in such formal surroundings on a daily basis – once a week like a Sunday lunchtime I can handle. . I asked where the crew ate. I felt Stu could handle the officer's mess better than I could and he probably had a napkin ring.

The crew's mess was down deck level, it was large enough to seat eighty people on fixed wooden bench-seats. The tables were covered with sunflower-patterned plastic covers. On each table, there was a double-loaf pile of hot fresh-baked bread and a big block of NZ butter.

The table by the entrance door was the centre of attention. It held two twenty-litre soup-pots full of borscht, which the crew dipped into as they passed. Paper towels were everywhere - slurping borscht can be messy in any sea conditions. For me borscht was a word and a dish that was a new experience, I took an instant liking to the name and feeding ritual.

"One is vegetarian and one has meat," said the pixie-faced mate while he was running a ladle through the borscht [as if panning for diamonds or something more valuable]. His dredging subjected him to good-natured repartee and low-blow insults delivered in accented English for our amusement. It was obvious he was popular, even though the crew thought the officers were 'the vermin' who ate all the meat. I asked where I could sit, if I used the crew mess and he replied unmistakably, "Anywhere."

A Small Digression ₒ ₒ ₒ ₒ

That night at `petit appetit`, I chose a wall seat with a view of the whole mess. When I asked the surly occupant to move it caused a chain reaction that probably registered on the Geiger counter two floors above. Mutterings went around the mess, as each man moved in some sort of pecking order. I felt good about my seat selection but no one else did.

We were shown our cabin. It had a porthole, and was on a deck level with the junior officers [protégés] and the senior supervisors. The cabin had under and over single bunks. Stu took the lower bunk because it was easier to fit the inner-sprung mattress he trucked from Taranaki. The new mattress was a little too wide but Stu was happy to sleep in the camber.

I checked out my bunk. The mattress wasn't soft [hotel comfort], but it was better than some I had slept on while working coastal boats.

The impish mate guided us down a long dimly lit passageway. The walkway was painted in a pale yellow and our progress was like a saunter in the moonlight, at the end of the corridor he introduced us to the laundry woman. She was surrounded by hillocks of wet laundry in a brightly lit room full of large stainless-steel machinery. I was dumbstruck by the size of her arms. They were *limboid-maximus*, enormous upper and lower muscles attached to hands that could hide a basketball. If the laundry machinery broke down, she would have no problems doing the washing by hand. She was in sole charge of the laundry for the crew of eighty.

"Level three, Tuesday, all washing" she said with a pleasant accented voice

Stu said, "They pull the sheets out from under you if you don't put them out to wash on the day they want them." He was flirting with the washerwoman, flashing his best come-on smile. He was the only man I knew, who could have done that [and got away with it]. She postured disdainfully with the massively muscular hands of toil and returned the eye contact. You could see the man from Wheramoamoa had her attention.

Stu was resourceful. He was a man who could break a gate in half, and then, half fix it in a hurry. He was a man who flirted with any woman, undaunted by size or conventional beauty. He managed to get the laundress` name from the guide and used it as often as he could, he was on a charm siege, but she just smiled pleasantly and said, "Level three, Tuesday, all washing."

We were shown the shower room. It was obvious it doubled as a delousing chamber and the lead linings suggested it could be used for a radiation wash down. At the centre, under micro-jets of water a group of naked men were soaping each other down while the cleaning lady mopped the floor in front of them.

The cleaning woman's size and swabbing action made the passageway impassable [and risky]. She was a colossal woman [giantess XOS], twice the size of laundry-lady, yet she was muscularly proportioned, in a steroid sort of way. Stu was in love again and he struck up an eye-play with her too.

At that point, I was ready for anything. These women were very large and very friendly. I asked the interpreter how many women were on the vessel. The answer was four,: a cook, a cleaner, a washer, and a server [in the officer's mess]. Stu panted, "Last time on was on the boat our server was pretty."

Our tour progressed to an incredibly clean fish factory, it had the mixed odours of industrial sanitizer and deodorizers and there, I realized I wasn't the oldest person on the boat. It was geriatric-ville on the lower decks, *'everyone was old and beyond'*. While I came to grips with that thought, a set of five eighty-year olds came through a floor-hatch from the bowels of the boat. Age showed on their faces and they were stooped, but they legged over the hatch coaming with sprightliness on their way to the mess.

We finished the tour at the doctors surgery. The doctor was middle aged, with a pleasant manner and good English. He looked me in the eye and said, "You should stop smoking."

Louisville Ridge - [2002] ○ ○ ○ ○

The Sapun Gora crew worked twelve-man shifts throughout the night to complete the wire. It was a job to be done quickly needed two wire rollers on the wharf and the crew winding port and starboard winches simultaneously

We had meetings with the bridge officers [hatchet men with nautical ranks] and another with the captain. Stu had told me they resented our presence and it showed with their false smiles and hesitant eye contact. The treatment we got wasn't nice but it was bearable. At the time, the Kursk Submarine tragedy occupied the thoughts and conversations of the Ukrainian officers. Many of the dead had been friends and acquaintances of the *Sapun* Gora crew.

The captain was thickset and he had the manner of a street brawler. His deck officers became servile in his presence. Except for the interpreter the officers were testimony to high carbo-loadings and little exercise. Stories of near mutiny are common when these ships are discussed but the captain appeared to be in command of a very tight ship.

We sailed after the morning meetings. There was no chitchat or polite conversation in the wheelhouse when we left our berth. The bridge became an 'orders only' precinct. The nautical orders were relayed from pilot to helmsman through the interpreter. Then a high-level bridge officer reported the helmsman had repeated the order correctly. When the vessel cleared the outer harbour, we gave the captain a course to steer. He immediately told the helmsman and he told the radio operator, who in turn told people ashore. It became obvious a chain-of-command drove the vessel. There would be no secrets on this trip as our every move would be relayed shore-side.

We went to the seamount at 37°south first, because we knew there was a school of fish there that hadn't been harvested. We were uneasy about it because previous trips had been fizzers, firstly with the blown Turbo on the *Santa Monica* and then the 'no show' on the *Seamount Explorer* trip.

We arrived at the 37°south seamount in early June and there were three iceboats working the grounds when we got there and they were coming to the end of their trips. Typically, the iceboats can spend up to ten days on the grounds. These vessels [*Pacific Bounty*, *Baldur*, and *Ocean Reward*] headed to the seamount early that season. 'Too early', is a constant cry, from people involved in a seasonal fishery. When the *ice boats* left the seamount, we could search without deception and shoot without waiting or warning. Stu started the equivalent of trawl strafing, that is, we towed our net over the points of interest from every angle possible, around-the-clock.

There were no fish marks to shoot. We just kept shooting the gear and we towed until we became stuck, or ran out of wire. We came fast over a hundred times '*on end*'. Sometimes we travelled a mile in reverse to get back over the gear and the sea birds [which normally fly ahead of the vessel] quickly changed their habit and waited patiently for us to come back to them

At the start of our trawl bombardment, the Ukrainian deck crew got excited when we hooked up. They watched from safe perches as knee-high waves rushed down the deck. They broke into excited chatter when sea spouts came to life, propelled by two-and-a-half thousand tons of boat butting a flat transom against the seas chop.

Experience makes kiwi Roughy fishermen the best in the world and Stu had 'hook-up' experience. The net hooked up a hundred and eleven times [Keith the observer recorded it].

Kiwi skippers are good at reading sounders and assessing the nature of the seafloor to avoid the sticky ground. The hook-ups had the captain showing heighten anxiety. It is a big job to keep a big boat and a net on target and it needs teamwork and fear, the fear of letting the team down and the captain got gripped by it. Sweat poured from his forehead in rivulets and he used a very large and impressive, spotlessly clean handkerchief to wipe his sweat-rivers and he did it every day, twice a day, in four hour shifts.

The Captain was the third man sitting on the couch and was seated close to the helmsman. He barked numbers that represented courses, wire speed, wire length and boat speed. He got the speeds and wire length from Stu, who was working from the net-monitor and the courses from my curser read-out on the plotter. Our fishing involved towing a rollover bank and Stu was trying to find new ways down its rugged sides. Things snagged, doors fell over and net damage couldn't be avoided.

The Ukrainians weren't used to net damage. Their mid-water nets were low maintenance because there was no seafloor contact. The deck crew complained about net mending. Hearing deck crew complaining isn't unusual, but on a kiwi roughy boat the crew never complains about net mending. Someone said with jest, and some seriousness,

"Ukrainian women are good net menders." Mishka, the net

master was horrified when we asked them to lace up the torn mesh instead of mending it properly. He described the practice, with words our dictionary translated as '*mafia town*'.

We fished the seamount relentlessly and learnt the angles and coral patches. All deep-water bottom-trawlers avoid trawling coral grounds. Coral will wreck nets and break ground-gear, and worst of all, its dead weight can bugger the lifting machinery. The coral grounds of the Louisville are intact.

The *Sapun Gora* was Meridian class and these vessels have a Heath Robinson system for freezing the fish down. It was a combination of mechanical chain-drives, hydraulics, and compressed air. The snap-freezing system had two processing belts. Each belt held over a thousand fish trays, it was over capacity for fish we were landing. Our average shot had been a tonne and we were using about twenty trays each time we hauled. The freezing system was so big that it took two days for fish to complete their passage through the system.

Every night there was a ritual, whereby the factory-foreman arrived at the wheelhouse with the completed daily tally sheet. He passed the handwritten totals to the factory manager who disappeared into an office cabin and re-appeared with typed paperwork. The typed paper was then signed and witnessed by both foreman and manager. The factory manager passed the typed page, with a grunt [Ukrainian], to the senior bridge-officer. The officer perused it and with a deeper grunt, passed it to the captain, who did a read and grunt, paused [theatrically] and then shook it [impatiently] in the air for the underling of the moment to pluck it out of his hands. We witnessed this ritualistic chain of grunts on a daily basis.

The paperwork was passed on to the senior radio officer. The radio officer continued the process of 'read and grunt' before retiring to one of the radio rooms and sending the details onto the shoreside management.

An Extraneous bit about the Dunnies ○○○○

When I recounted my experiences about fishing on the Soviet trawler everyone wanted to know about the toilets. Stories about the toilets on foreign boats are mostly horror stories and on the first look inside one, it is obvious the stories have foundation. On our deck level, there was one male dump station for over thirty people and there was always a queue of three or more outside at peak times. The far corner of the closet had a bucket filled with pungent milky disinfectant and a swabbing-mop. The toilet was the squatter with a hole in the deck head which breathed laboriously like a blowhole with pleurisy. A mop was rammed down the hole to stop users from being covered in blowback.

The holes mouth had a plinth of earthenware pipe. When the boat rolled the emanating stench of uric acid combined with mature compost permeated over the powerful disinfectant for a moment or two. The metre-by-three-metre-room was painted battleship grey. Haste was the essence of a blowhole visit and the queue moved along at a steady rate.

There weren't any bleach issues with the toilet paper. The A4 flat sheets were barely processed, and you could be forgiven for thinking you were using a pot scrubber when you used them.

Against the back wall, a latticed galvanized-wire bin held the same paper, now graphically soiled. Amongst it, a platoon [marine] of scurrying cockroaches played in the shit-stained mess looking for treats. Every morning the used paper was handed over with a deck door ritual [not unlike a border crossing] from the great arms of the cleaning lady to the deck crew, who then burnt it in a forty-gallon drum incinerator welded to the back quarterdeck. Old engine oil was used to combust the shitty mess and. the smell of the smoke was a repulsive morning wake up.

Early in the trip, Stu started using the women's toilet. He said it smelt better and he liked its bright colours. The women's loo had a cross bar with a plastic padded seat. The massive cleaning lady [*giantess XOS*] sprung him using it and was not happy. She became an irate half-tonne of angry human and any thought of a love affair was off. Stu gave her some *deluxe* NZ toilet paper [three ply]. He promised her a six-pack every week. The bribe calmed her down and he continued to use her bog without hindrance.

A Hundred Tonnes of Product o o o o

We were catching fish in small parcels but the roes didn't appear to be ripening. We needed a break for a sleep catch up because the non-stop fishing had exhausted us. We'd slept while the gear was being hauled and we were woken when it was five hundred metres deep on the next predetermined tow. We were getting an hour of sleep every four hours and we had been on this sleep pattern for three weeks. It had been hard work mentally, but the reward was a payload. We had caught a hundred tonnes of fish and we had heard a lot of grunts to get those hundred tonnes of Roughy[1] but we were probably the only ones pleased with the results – fishing had been slow.

We now had a pay and it allowed us to gamble, so we went cruising to see if we could find a big mark and get the giant factory system working to the max. We headed south to the 38°30s seamount and there we did a long tow to determine the state of the roes in the area.

The fish we caught had advanced roes, but the eggs weren't separated, meaning they were a fortnight to a month away from a spawn school-up. There was no holding back the man from Wheramoamoa; he was the same man who had invented '*drive-by Roughy shooting*'.

---

[1] All the lower level crew knew the totals - they keep their own tally because they had all been ripped off in the past

When catches are slim, 'drive-by' is a chance to catch up on sleep. We steamed the days and fished the nights as we *hill hopped*. It was seamount hopping with hope. Hope is held in the clasp of old gullies and peaks that produced catches in the past even though we would be 'drive-by' fishing them at historically bad times.

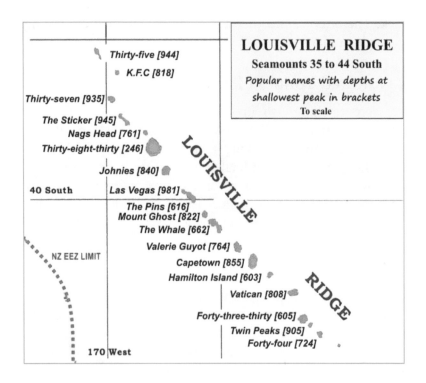

We ordered a course to start our drive-by down the Louisville Ridge. The captain ordered full-speed ahead and the vessel speed up to an impressive fourteen knots. The old spots of yester-year: The Whale, DPB, Scarface, Dodge, Ghost, and Capetown were associated with good catches [and nostalgia] but on the drive-by, they produced meagre returns.

After a week we decided the drive-by tour was a waste of time and we headed back to the 38°30s seamount [where we started and seen the best roes].

On the 28 June 2002, the officers celebrated what they said was *"Ukrainian Fishermen's Constitution Day"* and we learnt it had been a venerable celebration since 1996. The celebration was a time for the officers to get drunk and the crew to get jealous. Two of the protégés were left on watch and the rest of the upper deck swanned drunkenly around them.

We heard the history of Sebastopol. We heard of a yearlong siege when Sebastopol fought the French, British, Turks, and Sardinians [at the same time].

We were getting a bit tired of siege stories, but the history lessons flowed. They boasted democracy since 400BC [watching the wheelhouse carousal going on, it seemed democracy was 'only a guideline']. They were sacked by the Tatars, when the Tatars were a power and although it happened hundreds of years ago, they remembered it.

I wanted to tell them about Tuhawaiki storming north from Ruapuke to repel attacks on the South Island but it was a night for tales about *'olde Sevastopol'*. There, where the Navy engaged in mutiny [with a big M in 1905] and there where the last stand of White Russia had happened.

We heard of another siege lasting eight months fighting the Germans at the end of WW2. We heard the last week of the defence had been done doggedly from the rubble remains of the city, and there were thousands of enemy killed.

The officers loved the city [with adoration]. They were proud of their history and the fact they were part of Sebastopol. It was a city, they said, they would proudly die for and they didn't mind repeating the statement.

The officers were graduates of the Black Sea Higher Naval Institute and they were broadly educated. The Constitution Day celebrations were emotive yet delicate. I admired them for the way they went about it – eight people did the celebrating for the other seventy. It was easy to experience growing insecurities as the officers progressed to aggressive drunkenness and started reliving past glories with animation. It was also easy to slope away unnoticed.

When we arrived back at the 38°s seamount, we did a bank-tow and the tow showed scratches and marks on the monitor. The cod-end produced a tonne of fish with running roe suggesting the fish were spawning somewhere close-by and we hoped it wouldn't take long to find the spawn aggregation.

That night, in the crew's mess there was a feast of fresh Orange Roughy roe. The roe was spread on 'doorsteps' of fresh bread and the word 'caviar' accompanied grins and gluttony.

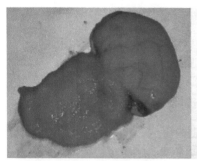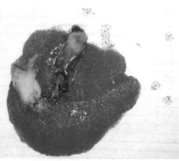

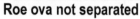

Roe ova not separated   **Ripe and ova running**

When we found the fish aggregation, they were spawning five nautical miles from where the previous spawn had been. The new spawn area was deeper and in a siding valley beside a rock pile. It was a typical spawn spot, with side-echo and mud to confuse echo-signals [and predators]. There was a nearby pinnacle for egg distribution and a salient and a canyon facing a major upwelling from the abysmal sea depths.

Within a short time we put a hundred tonnes in the hold and the vessel was working *'maxed out with a bag on deck'*.

We were starting to dream and feel excited but that evening during the factory-tally ritual, things didn't change. The fish factory was in full swing but the chain of grunting during the factory-figure hand-over, just seemed wearier.

After the second day of good catches and following the formalities of the daily catch reporting, the tired chain-of-grunts was replaced with animated conversation and busy footsteps. The bridge officers were in conference and the stoic faces were replaced with open smiles [for the first time that trip]. We thought we were about to get pats on the back and thanks for the catch. We were on top of the world, wearing winners' grins and experiencing relief.

Then we received the mother of all bombshells. The boat, our interpreter explained, must head back to Lyttleton immediately because the hoki season had started. We were required to break off our hunt at the harvest stage. Deflation ruled and we took its punch with capitulation. The new plan cost us a certain pay bonanza.

The Ukrainian crew were happy because they got a better bonus for hoki fishing and it was the reason they came to New Zealand.

That night when I went to the mess, the Ukrainian crewman [whose seat I'd taken at the start of the trip] beamed at me from his old perch, suggesting unmovable defiance. It was not a time to argue I took a seat at the old man's table by the galley door and started a bowl of borscht. A front-line kitchen-marine, like a character from a soviet classic story appeared and served me pastry treats. I felt honoured and humble but then I realized that all the old boys were served pastry treats as a reward [for age] and I'd been at the wrong table the whole trip.

The ship's doctor [who sat centre table] told me I wasn't the only one who found my situation amusing and I reflected how eating with foreign crews always seemed to lead me to embarrassment.

***

If Stu hadn't been so good at doing it, I could have treated frustration by punching walls but Stu's wall punching skills had the benefit of a decade of karate lessons. The Ukrainian kick boxing champion [who practised outside in any sea or weather] said he thought Stu, '*punctured steel very good*'. He offered Stu his heavy workout bag but Stu didn't let up on his wall punching sessions.

The wheelhouse had calmness; the Ukrainian officers were winding down. They were taking turns at being the loser for a captain who liked playing '*pin ball*' on the ships computer.

I wasted time solving cryptic crosswords composed by a friend [Rex], who uses the pseudo-de-plume *Kropotkin*. I think the name is homage to things anarchistic from Rex`s university days. Before long, I had an audience looking over my shoulder. The oncoming bridge officers were sure I was doing the real Professor Kropotkin's puzzles. They had spied Rex`s by-line and thought the puzzles were those of the famous geographer who they had studied at Nautical School. An English speaking protégé started relaying the clues and answers were proffered.

Stu kept bashing walls though and he had started kicking things and swearing. He had reason enough but it had the officers looking sideways and the Ukrainian kickboxing champion moved his training area onto the wheelhouse roof.

When the factory crew had finished cleaning the vessel, they changed the situation by visited Stu and they all had photos of blonde women. They assailed Stu with them.

The picturesque blondes had smiles and comely looks and yes, they would marry a backcountry farmer in New Zealand. The 'blonde-photos' weren't lewd. They were best-side shots and the women pictured were the daughters and relatives of the crew. Stu`s mind was released from its disappointed state.

"Get my Filo-fax" was his order, I obeyed, and it was the last order Stu gave that trip. He copied names, pronunciations, phone numbers, and addresses all day.

When the massive cleaning lady came to see Stu, he copied down her details and gave her the inner sprung mattress he trucked from the Taranaki. They smiled at each other wickedly and Stu gave her the last packs of 3-ply super soft. There were things the man from Wheramoamoa might follow up on because his address book was full

10...Baldur

Nelson –July [2003] ₀ ₀ ₀ ₀

The Sapun Gora trip should have been a bonanza but that didn't happen. We had been in position where we had a massive spawn mark and no competing boats within cooee.

When I thought about it, I was liable to mutter [loudly] *"And we had a big boat, a big crew, and a big freezer."* The spawning fish would disappear before we could return [the Roughy roes told the story].

It was a low point. All I could do was nail down the starting blocks and wait for my luck to change. It was a short wait and began a wonderful run of fishing - *an orange purple-patch* I liked to call it [in a Jackson Bay kind-of-way]. At Jackson Bay, they love mixing colours, metaphors, malapropisms, and alliteration. They enjoy the sounds of the words; it's the language [almost childish] of remote areas and probably an early sign of cabin fever.

The good run of good luck, began with a phone call from skipper Heals [*Santa Monica*] offering a trip to the bottom of the Louisville Ridge. He had managed to get hold of me before I docked from the *Sapun Gora* trip. When you get job offers before you hit the wharf, it's safe to presume there's desperation involved and you weren't the first person to get the offer.

We would be heading to the 46°s east seamount, known as *Aussies* or the *500 tonne hill* because of the tonnage Aussie [Clifford] said he caught there. He had been skippering the vessel Kermadec and was probably telling the truth.

Paul [Hendry] worked Aussies hill before he went to fish in Tristan De Cuna [on the *San Liberatore*] and he had gaven his fish positions to our vessel's owners

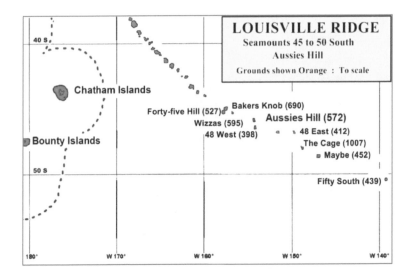

We sailed at the end of July and our trip was a successful hundred-tonne catch. We fished spawn-fish at shallow depths [600 metres]. It seemed, the further south we fished, the higher up the water column the fish spawned and presumably, the water temperatures dictated it.

Baldur ○ ○ ○ ○

Hori, the skipper of the *Baldur* offered me a job. He sniffed we had a mark – sniffing out marks is one of his strong points. Some call him 'the Maori hypnotist' because of it. The job he offered was four weeks on and ten days off, for two years. There were other details suggesting planning was afoot. The areas of operations included North Island's East Coast and the Chatham Rise with seasonal fishing at the Louisville Ridge and the Challenger Plateau.

Doing Chatham Island circuits for a year or two was appealing. Satellite-imagery of the Chatham Rise showed it had the highest density of life anywhere on the planet and that was good enough reason to take the job.

The Rise is a massive undersea plateau. In area it is as big as the entire South Island of New Zealand Put another way, it is bigger than the Grand Banks of New Foundland and the North Sea Dogger Bank of Britain put together.

The Baldur's name suggested a relationship to Odin and Thor and it conjured up thoughts of Vikings and North Sea cod wars. It was German built for fresh fish trawling in the North Sea and could haul a hundred and fifty tonnes of whole-fish on board in less than two days with a small crew. The Baldur's ice-class hull could punch a big sea and its flair could split the roughest seas around the bow sides. Its decks drained in an instant.

FV Baldur   LOA 38.95 metres GT 299

Baldur was built to take advantage of the rules for vessels less than forty metres in length. These vessels have lower port charges and for most ports, pilots were not needed for harbour manoeuvres. The manning regulations for under forty-metre vessels required three officers [skipper, mate, and chief engineer]. This is a cost saving because vessels just five centimetres longer require twice as many officers and engineers. She was designed by naval architects who understood the needs of fishermen who worked rough seas.

The Baldur's buoyancy provided a stable deck in any sea, and the more fish you put in the holds the better it handled the weather. The deck had double sweep drums with a separate net-roller. The set-up meant there was the choice of three nets ready to go fishing at any time.

The Baldur had been a North Sea basher for twenty years before the Muollo family bought and refitted it. At the time [2003], boats built for the North Sea made up most of New Zealand's deep-sea fleet, and they always seemed to have initial problems when they came to the southern oceans. Soft iron [magnetics] and a history of limited maintenance were the main causes for them needing work.

The North Sea bashers lived on in New Zealand because of the Kiwi engineers who manned them. The typical Kiwi engineer is a resourceful person who is able to get power from A to B in a breakdown situation and do it in a hurry [and stop a skipper's swearing recital]. Mechanical or fluid-power breakdowns stop catches coming aboard or disabled the auxiliary machinery needed to convey the fish or keep it chilled.

A forty-metre chief engineer is a welder, electrician, plumber, cook, and household appliance fixer. He can make a grappling hook in an instant and fix a radar-scanner bearing in the nastiest of seas. Good engineers are 'miracle workers' in situations where there is a valuable catch [with a short shelf life] at stake.

By 2003, *Baldur* was a successful boat in the Cook Strait Hoki fishery. Baldur had fished the Challenger grounds and it had been revitalized by a succession of good engineers [Rodger, Punga and Rabbit]. The credit for its good catching record should go to the Baldur's skipper Charlie [Rees], whose name is normally super-glued to the words 'lucky' and 'bastard'.

Baldur's bottom fishing nets were different from those most trawlers had on-board.

As the story goes, the vessel *Giuseppe's* bridge-officers, in need of a net [after destroying its Roughy nets], had tried a squid net as a substitute. The squid net was a remnant of another venture. There remains a historic friendly dispute as to who suggested it, which often occurs with innovation. Paul [Hendry] was skipper at the time and skippers always get credit for these things, although the net innovation became known as the *Larry* net.

Squid nets have very little headline opening, they could be likened to an eels mouth and they are designed to fish hard down. The squid net was a 'left field thought' because high lift head-lines were in fashion at the time. The outcome of the squid-net gamble was a Roughy catch and little net damage.

It was a thing that impressed Lorrie [from Stewart Island] and when he was employed on Baldur, he requested two nets made to resemble the squid-net proportions.

The new nets were strengthened and designed to suit Baldur's horsepower. It was the first innovation in the Roughy fishery since the Fifeshire/Whitby wingless nets were developed by the Sealord skippers a decade and a half before.

When the *Larry net* came fast, it presented a minimum of loose mesh to the seafloor because there were no side panels to fold over and it helped that the mesh that might snag on the seafloor was double twine.

Cod ends full of fish on Baldur deck the result of a fifty second trawl using the Larry net [seen from winch drivers station]

The fish seemed to want to go in the net rather than be pushed. On most occasions, we got only one good shot at a fish mark, such was its effectiveness. Perhaps it was an absence of pressure waves, or maybe its low-mouth invited fish to enter the confines. Whatever the reason, it worked!

The *Larry net* ground rig was virtually a 300mm thick rubber band with a heavy chain core. It was a ground hugger and capable of being rolled around the net-roller drum for easy shoot and haul operations.

Ruru Rescue - April [2003] ₀ ₀ ₀ ₀

In April 2003, a nasty storm system in the Tasman Sea had us 'dodging in the ditch' at the bottom of the Challenger Plateau. We'd had slow fishing before the storm and the first two days of dodging seemed like a week in time.

Slow fishing can send a crew into a morose mood and with a bit of dodging time added, some of the crew were coming to the end of their civilised behaviour. It seemed likely the gym equipment would be smashed or slashed.

The Tasman Sea was being ploughed by a wave-cyclone, a depression caused by sea-level low-pressure systems being trapped between high-pressure zones. Anti-cyclonic air masses feed the cyclones storm centre. The centre surfs along the walls of the high-pressure zones on a meridian track while spitting out fronts. This type of storm is a common occurrence in the Tasman Sea and the word 'sea' suggests nasty frontal weather. The upwelling sea currents [at the fishing grounds] intensify the forces. There are times when giant waves break leaving nothing but white-water in their wake. The low-pressure systems are called 'sea bombs' when they wash out a coastal landfall.

Late on the third night of dodging, our communication system started making the noises associated with some sort of sea disaster. Flashing lights and shrill alarms demanded attention. Messages had to be printed and ACK-buttons pressed several times to quieten the wheelhouse. The 'Immarsat' messages requested 'all vessels in our area to report their positions'.

Emergency broadcasts coming through the wire service from places 'global-wide' are common [the new electronics have seen to it], but it's rare to get one concerning your vessel. This time it was our turn to take part in a sea rescue. A stricken vessel [yacht] was in a position seventy miles from our location and it would take us over ten hours of punching the weather to reach the yacht.

The dangerous thing about Tasman depressions is the associated frontal-winds are constantly changing direction relative to a boat's course. If the boat gets side-on for too long, all hell breaks loose and out of shipshape. To keep a vessel on course during the fury requires vigilance, trusty electronics, and a good autopilot. There is always the thought you might have to hand-steer using the compass. Things breakdown in storms - it's a fact! Baldur's thousand horsepower was made for quick course changes, - something that can't be done on a two-knot yacht. The stricken vessel had been blown apart while it was over the shallow line fishing grounds which is also an area of very strong upwellings.

Yacht masters should check the ocean charts before starting their voyages. They should be able to identify fishing grounds on the chart because the fishing grounds are likely to have large steel trawlers [with AIS off] and fishing grounds are where the real bad weather is. They are the surge ponds of the Abysmal Sea.

Our course from *Easy Street* to the stricken yacht's position had us transiting a closed fishing area. This area is a fishing industry agreement to protect an area of Orange Roughy spawn activity. Fishing is automatically monitored for boats in the closed zone by satellite polling.

There are two closed areas off New Zealand – the other is on the Chatham rise. The transit meant we had to notify the Fishery Control Centre [FCC] giving times and positions of entry and departure from the zone.

Our departure from the closed area would take us from outside to inside the NZ EEZ and this required more reporting. It was an operation with paperwork. We couldn't help thinking a transit button would have been handy during such an emergency which required detailed half-hourly reporting.

We had just entered the closed area when the search was called off [we weren't given a reasons why]. These rescue operations can cause 'pay-pain' on a fresh-fish trawler. The margins involved do not allow for indiscriminate steaming over the ocean. On our boat, everyone was paid with a catch-share and grumpiness started permeating.

We set a course back to the fishing seamounts but three hours up the track, another message from *Search & Rescue* asked us to once again go to the rescue. Entrance and exit faxes to FCC were promulgated, once more.

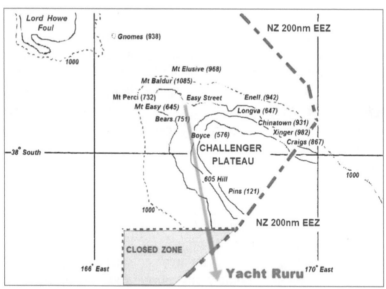

Challenger Seamounts and the course to crippled yacht 'Ruru'

Noon arrived and we were two hours away from the vessel when an air force Orion did a radio check on the VHF radio. They were leaving Manukau and the Orion's radio operator had been loud and clear, from 350 nautical miles away. The Orion had a good horizon factor for its VHF transmissions. Within minutes, we could hear the Orion's communications with the yacht although we could only hear the Orion-side of the conversation.

There was a debate going on and the air-force captain was offering the yacht`s skipper three alternatives. The yacht could continue under their own steam; the people could abandon the vessel and board us; or they could abandon and accept a tow from us. The yacht`s captain was having trouble making his mind up. What he had thought might happen after he set off his EPIRB was difficult to imagine. While we waited for his decision, the Orion radio officer relayed *Black Cap* scores from an exciting cricket game helping to lighten the situation.

The yacht-master decided to abandon his vessel but he was anxious we tow the damaged sailboat to port. The yacht was a thirty-foot concrete-hulled vessel of some age. The mast had fallen through the wheel house-roof [stepped down], after the forward stays had broken. A message came through from our management warning us the yacht's owner was bankrupt and had been the subject of deep-sea rescues on two previous occasions.

We took the old yacht [Ruru] undertow. Tow ropes often break when unavoidable chaffing happens at the tethers It is a sea rule, `always use the towed boat's rope and get them to accept Lloyds open form`. In other words, you use their rope because yours will be damaged or you won't get it back at the completion of the tow. Lloyds open form covers a salvage vessel from most contingencies.

The yacht crew were young German back-packers having their first ocean experience and they were hungry. When we offered them steak, eggs and chips, they protested [in good English] that they were vegetarians and after declining our offer, they went back to talking in German. It was an odd thing because fresh vegetables are always a problem at sea. On Baldur, Johnny [the cook] wrapped our fresh veges individually in newspaper to promote a longer-life.

We couldn`t help thinking their yacht must have been packed with mung beans, lentils and cabbages. Why hadn't the vegetarians, with their special need diets, brought any food at transfer time? Food is an important consideration in all abandon ship operations. The cook mixed fresh vegetables with frozen and gave them each a bowl of rice and a fresh cut fruit salad while our crew made short work of the steak!

The stricken yacht's pumps couldn't handle the water it was shipping. This was not helped by the damage done when the mast went through the battery-box. The rescued yachtsman related he was an out-of-work home-birth doctor and told us stories of woe [with resignation]. He hadn't wanted to abandon his yacht, but after using his two emergency beacons [EPIRB] he was forced to do so. His insurance did not cover ocean travel and he was sailing a rumb-line from Nelson to Sydney, Australia.

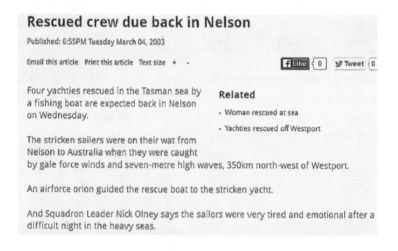

Rescued crew due back in Nelson

Published: 6:55PM Tuesday March 04, 2003

Email this article   Print this article   Text size +   -

Four yachties rescued in the Tasman sea by a fishing boat are expected back in Nelson on Wednesday.

Related

- Woman rescued at sea
- Yachties rescued off Westport

The stricken sailors were on their wat from Nelson to Australia when they were caught by gale force winds and seven-metre high waves, 350km north-west of Westport.

An airforce orion guided the rescue boat to the stricken yacht.

And Squadron Leader Nick Olney says the sailors were very tired and emotional after a difficult night in the heavy seas.

We lost the yacht off Farewell Spit – it slid into the depths with silence [still under-tow]. The towline was cut and we reported its final position to rescue headquarters, including the fifteen litres of fuel and oil it had in its tanks. [Fifteen litres didn't seem to be much fuel for a Tasman crossing]. When the Tasman Sea is moody, it is definitely no place for old yachts.

The Ruru rescue voyage turned out to be our only unsuccessful trip in the two years of fishing on the Baldur.

Roughy Warnings - [2003] ₒₒₒₒ

Doom documents were starting to appear in the mainstream press and on the second to last day of 2003, the WWF released a statement....

Rough Seas for Orange Roughy: Popular U.S. Fish Import in Jeopardy, Says World Wildlife Fund 12/30/03, Newswire
'Reckless overfishing [sic] is rapidly causing the demise of Orange Roughy and other imported fish species popular with US consumers, according to a new scientific study released by the World Wildlife Fund [WWF] and TRAFFIC. The study finds that rapidly expanding and unregulated fishing in deep waters is fast depleting species that could become commercially extinct if protective measures are not taken immediately by international governing bodies.
The report shows that "some deep ocean fish stocks, like Orange Roughy, have been wiped out in less than four years," said Simon Habel, director of TRAFFIC-North America, the wildlife trade-monitoring network. "As Americans buy more and more Orange Roughy, they contribute to the pressures that could ultimately take the fish right off their plates and out of the seas as well." The United States is a significant and growing market for Orange Roughy, importing more than 19 million pounds annually in recent years and accounting for nearly 90 percent of documented catches'.

The bit about taking the fish out of the seas seemed a bit over the top - WWF obviously didn't know how hard Orange Roughy were to track down and catch

Port Nicholson - April [2004] ₒₒₒₒ

Hori had always been able to keep a secret; he would have made a good secret agent if he hadn't been a fisherman.

He was a good winkler as well. In the two years we worked together, he had extracted all my fishing secrets with ease. We got on well; we shared a love for hunting fish and we were both optimistic about fill-ups.

We had an outstanding run of fishing for the two years we worked together and we shared *Red Moon*. Red Moon was a fishing seamount that could have inspired song. It was tucked away in the Lord Howe Foul ditch [up a siding]. It was a once in a lifetime occasion, an unfished seamount with fishing and the good weather caused the moon to have a red glow. Red moon had saved a fishing trip heading towards failure and it had engendered personal thanks from our boss.

I am not sure how long Hori had kept this secret, but finally he let out a hint he was privy to something I didn't know. Skipper / mate partnerships don't normally allow secrets like the one he was hinting at, "It was big," he said, but he couldn't tell me until we docked.

We were through the harbour heads when he repeated his knowledge of the secret. We had passed a brooding Barrett Reef and an active Breaker Bay, and we had the lead-lights in line. From that position, it would be an hour wait before he relieved my agitated curiosity.

"You'll never guess," he said and it twisted my brain. It was an invitation he knew I couldn't turn down.

"The cops are waiting on the wharf to arrest one of the crew?" I volunteered.

"That's not big." he said and his big grin grew to Golden Bay size.

It was a quantifier, I felt like arguing about. The phone rang; it was our boss and Hori said into the phone [loud enough for me to hear], "No, I haven't told anyone." He repeated it [with a little tee-hee], while looking at me with a victimizing look.

From where I was sitting, the situation was starting to smell like a `tease tasting`. Big secrets and phone calls from the big boss had me really thinking. The situation demanded nothing less than wild guesses and for me; wild guesses have never been a challenge. My guesses ranged from total quota cuts to catching fish in French Polynesia.

Guessing filled in the time, including the delays doing a '*Jerningham joggle*' waiting for a coastal container boat to shift at the Aotea Wharves. Hori was grinning all the time; he was being both rebutter and surrejoinder to my guesses.

When we were tied up, the secret came out. The boat and the fishing company had been sold to Ngāi Tahu. There were suited people on the wharf and they were driving Japanese cars, which was unusual at our berth, because our crew drove Ford or Holden and our management drove BMW.

I felt disappointed; I had expected salaciousness or skulduggery to accompany such a secret. Then I felt like a piece of the South Island, the bit with the widest part of the *long white cloud*, had come to visit.

A boat like Baldur changing hands was unusual. Tony [Muollo] had brought it from Helgi in Iceland [with secret ceremony] and the boat had been a big winner.

From the moment in time, the Baldur berthed at Aotea Quay number 5, would work for a company under the umbrella of Ngāi Tahu Fisheries and their nominees. Immediately our phone-list went from three to thirty-three numbers and names. Getting the new contact details onto our computer challenged our communication system, which at the time was barely out of its DOS diapers.

A family company with a management of three who were on hand twenty-four hours of the day, had grown into two companies full of university graduates. As time progressed, they became harder to track down than the fish we were trying to catch.

I'm a fourth generation South Island pakeha. My forebears lived on a hill between two fighting Pas [before their Treaty]. The tribes don't fight anymore both are part of Ngāi Tahu [but a good cockle bed is still worth bickering about].

With Ngāi Tahu, I have a sense of greater community, it is because I was a born South Islander and I spent considerable time in the company of the Bluff natives. If I'd known Ngāi Tahu were coming we would have flown bunting, stem to stern, every signal flag and ensign. It's a mates job to see to such things.

Baldur's wheelhouse filled up with people who had agendas. They were fresh shaven and wearing the type of leather shoes that were slippery on wharves and fishing vessels. They were enthusiastic and obliging, but they didn't want to leave the bridge.

On these occasions, a mate is busy with paperwork. You try to be polite locating pointless certificates and making hot drinks. There was a pile of paperwork, as you might imagine, with new Fishing Licenses being, *'from that moment and forthwith held on board,'* to satisfy legal requirements and quota laws. People wanted PTI's, insurance forms, manning certificates, survey forms, and in return they passed over business cards – frenetic exchanges of documents and details.

I snatched an embossed and monogrammed business card. Head office for our new owners was Christchurch - my birthplace. Christchurch - memories of the smell from stock-trucks stopped at the lights and slippery icy suburban streets, the smoggy skies and spring flowers, the memories flooded back invading my senses.

We did the rounds, handshakes and politeness prevailed.

"None of them are South Islanders," Hori exclaimed, when he ordered another coffee using his skipper's privilege. We had been hoping for a bit of gossip from down south. Just a titbit of 'real news' from the home island would have been nice, such as '*there's a new all-night service station at Cheviot'*, or '*there's a new B&B at Millers Flat'*.

If any of them had divulged some good rugby gossip, they would have gained a lifetime friend. News from the homelands makes a deep-sea fisher feel re-connected with a home-shore.

There must have been a time [I thought] when purchasing a boat Baldur's size would have meant something to Ngāi Tahu. It made good sense to have all those accountants, food scientists, and business analysts on board but nobody wanted a guided tour of the boat and we were all jammed in the wheelhouse being nice to each other. Baldur had been such a major part of the company's success and it was changing owners. It deserved more.

Public shareholder companies have ceremonies when commissioning a new acquisition and they roll out a Crown Minister [or two] when a new boat joins a fledgling fleet. Such an occasion should have had some ceremony. A few beers in the *Waterloo* on Wellington's waterfront would have been nice. Strip-teasers and lap dancers wouldn't have overdone the occasion.
'*Who needs ceremony? Ceremony - be damned!*'[1] *I thought*

The good fishing continued and we secured record catches for the new owners and controllers of protein and profit. We filled up twice at the Louisville Ridge and had a season of fishing [memorable for its abundance of fish, good pays, and reinforced friendships].

---

[1] In 2008 Ngāi Tahu sold *Baldur* to Chief Taiaroa Fisheries Ltd as a Chatham Island freighter.

11...A Decade at the Ridge

Wellington - [Ceremony - May 2004] ₀ ₀ ₀ ₀

Father Geoff [Broad] was on the back deck and a stiff breeze made his vestment robes billow out in front of him. He looked spiritual and he had learnt [at Island Bay] how to stand up-wind when there was Holy Water involved.

Our Indonesian crew [from Batang] would never have seen anything like Father Geoff in full voice. They went about their work with shy glances. The open leather-bound psalm book in Father Geoff's left hand oscillated within his depth of focus. His invocations to Stella Maris and Polaris were a relaxed performance, and at times, he directed them at our Muslim crew[1]. His blessing was a chance to think about things serious, the trip at hand, and fate. Father Geoff blessed the boat with a delivery that inspired hope. He was enthusiastic and the psalms gave him a chance to unleash his Latin language skills before he finished off in English.

Paraphrasing Father Geoff ₀ ₀ ₀ ₀

"Most gracious Lord, who numbered among your apostles the fishermen Peter, Andrew, James, and John, we pray you to consecrate this boat to righteously work in your name".

---

[1] Two of the Indonesian crew were bacon and egg loving Christians.

168

"We beseech you that the vessel has bountiful catches for the owners and so prosper her voyages that an honest living may be made".

"We pray you guide the captain at her helm. Watch over her crew and bring them to a safe return".

"The blessing of God Almighty, the Father, the Son and the Holy Spirit, be upon this vessel and all who come aboard, this day and forever. Amen"...Our *amens* [loud yet subdued] echoed after him and the reiterations started genuine smiles.

The big boat being blessed was the *San Liberatore*. It was freshly painted, but the hull showed numerous bumps and dents from thirty years of dockings and wharf-rub. The *San Lib* was built in 1972 at Bremerhaven [Germany]. Fishing people [worldwide] talked about the launching, as others would talk about the birth of a royal child. One of our factory managers [George] said he remembered the occasion well. At the time, he was employed in the sixty vessel Polish fishing fleet [with sub-Spartan living conditions] and he was envious.[1]

In 1972, the *San Lib* was launched as Hannover [with two n`s]. It had leather upholstery, steward call-buttons, showers with mixers and self-tuning TV aerials...and cruise ship comfort. Two MAK 1770 kW engines powered it. The hull-lines were exaggerated and shaped to push water to a single propeller [no nozzle]. It was heavily ribbed and it had survived a mid-ship ramming.

The San Lib had a nautical surety about its design and the brawn to handle big catches. The San Lib had a four door, fifty-tonne fish-pound backing onto a fish factory capable of producing fifty tonnes of product a day [and fishmeal from the offal].

---

[1] The Polish fleet had been decimated from sixty to three vessels by 2004.

San Liberatore "*slipped on the hard*" at Grand Canaria

An aside about Modern Factory Ships ₀ ₀ ₀ ₀

Nowadays there's automated mega-sized trawlers that can process 200 tonnes of product a day, but you wouldn't go Roughy hunting in them. Running costs limit the size of Roughy boats and vessels the size of the San Lib, are as big as it gets.

San Lib had been built for the Labrador fishery and was part of a family of trawlers working the fishery until it became uneconomic. The Hannover's documentation showed Cuxhaven and Kingston as past ports of Registry. Maritime records had it fishing off Africa, where it was known as `Seaflower`. It had completed fishing stints in the Indian, Atlantic and Pacific Oceans on its way to New Zealand. Twenty years of hard deep-sea work combined with stingy maintenance schedules had taken a toll on the vessel while it was based in Africa

The Hannover was renamed *San Liberatore* when the Vinnaccia and Muollo families bought it at the beginning of 2000. The new name celebrated the life of Liberatore Vinnaccia, a Wellington fishing identity.

San Lib was converted for use as a long-liner and sent chasing Toothfish in the Antarctic waters. It was ice strengthened when it was built for the Labrador fishery. *"There is no actual universal definition of what needs to be done to a ship for it to be 'officially ice strengthened' It can be applied to all manner of ships, whether supply ships, tankers, container ships, warships etc. Commonly ice-strengthened ships can cope with continuous one year old ice about 50cm - 100cm thick."*

The Toothfish venture had been a moderate success with adventures for all the crew. Video cameras had recorded Leopold Seals stealing 100 kg fish off the line and there were clips of the boat pushing huge icebergs aside to retrieve the fishing lines underneath them. Long lining was a job the boat hadn't been designed to do. First officer Hoy described manoeuvring it *"like driving a tennis court with an under-powered outboard engine."* Skipper Hendry reckoned, if they went to the ice again, they should put a Hamilton-jet on its bow as a thruster.

I joined *San Lib* after it returned from the Antarctic ice. It had been in the hands of kiwi engineers for two years by that time. Mechanical parts had been repaired to good working order and hundreds of light-fittings repaired or replaced. Good lighting is important on any boat. The bigger the boat, the darker its bowels become – anyone who has been on a dead ship or two will verify this.

San Lib's twelve engine cylinders, each 450mm bore with a half a metre of stroke, had been reconditioned to the manufacturer's specifications. Rust had been chipped and painted several times over and the vessel was showing the signs of care and wise expenditure.

My job as mate required the preparation of customs details, work rosters, and musters lists.

It was a task because of the similar names: Mahomet, Mahammed, Mahommed, Mehammad, Mochammad, Mohamed, Mohammad, Mohammed, Muhammad, Muhommad and Muhammed. It took considerable effort to sort out the M`s and wasn`t helped by spell-checker wanting to correct the names to 'Mohomed'. Reference books proffered the various spellings reflected a colonial past. It was little wonder the crew preferred to use any of their names not starting with M.

Musters and drills were according to the textbook and quick. The Indonesians readily taught new crew all the skills and procedures needed on the vessel. They chose their own leaders and showed judgment in doing so.

Chooks were a major providore item. We had a thousand [frozen] size 20's on board for the trip. They were stacked carefully, hogging the best freezer space. They were accompanied by a twenty-tonne staple of rice. "They would eat chicken every day if they could," Glenn, the factory manager told us when we discussed the 'Indo-crew'.

San Lib's bridge officers had been part of Roughy hunts all over the world and they were leading inshore-skippers before they went far-ocean fishing. Our engineers had worked on everything between glow-plugs and dump-valves, but the vessel was still 'work in progress', with heavy engineering work going on around the clock. Twenty-year-old refrigeration systems are a headache, whether they have been maintained or not. When the freezers weren't getting deep surgery, the giant fishmeal plant was being dismantled.

We made a master plot of the Louisville Ridge, which incorporated ten years of discoveries. The plot displayed contours, tows with times, positions for hook-ups, fish marks and lost gear. While we made the plot it was easy to reflect on the decade, we had spent at the Louisville Ridge.

All the seamounts had a 'lost' set of gear on them, most of which had been lost in the early days of the Louisville Ridge exploration. Fine tuning sounders and more accurate-plotting would have averted most of the losses but new tows in new fisheries are hurried. The sea-floor fissures [the crevices of misfortune] that snag the nets are often hard to detect before a hook-up, even though they stand out like glacial canyons [on the depth sounder] after the misfortune. It's an 'angle and gain' thing and the memory of a bad hook-up never fades.

The master plot revealed that some spawn spots had shifted about four miles over the decade. The fish had been pushed sideways to secondary spawning areas possibly because the substrate had been scraped away [losing its prawn base], or the aqua-dynamics of gullies had changed because the oceans push had changed.

There are still new spawn spots to be found at the Ridge, but for these areas to be uncovered, it would require a capital outlay that does not exist within the NZ fishing fraternity. A new spawn area would probably take three seasons to find and only just pay its way on today's prices.

Whales and Roughy Globally ₒ ₒ ₒ ₒ

Toothed Whales[1] put Roughy under pressure by predation and by feeding on the same food source [squid]. Whaling occurred big time in the early 20th century with the construction of large factory/mother ships and flotillas of catcher boats. The expansion ended in 1950 with *Olympic Challenger*, a vessel controlled by Aristotle Onassis was crewed with the best Norwegian whalers.

Olympic Challenger was the biggest whaler in the world. It was a converted oil tanker[2] and it was accompanied by seventeen corvettes [ex British and Canadian war issue]. The captain had been called "scruple-less" and he was an ostracized Nazi collaborator. He proved his lack of scruples by starting the season early and hunting whales previously protected by international law [and the whaler's code]. *The Challenger* had an extermination attitude.

Olympic Challenger had been hard at work for three years until a stint of poaching in Peruvian waters got them *sequestered*. Sequestration was something Onassis had $30,000 per day insurance to cover. Moreover, he had the cover for 7 October -

---

[1] Odontocete : Mainly Sperm Whale
[2] Its conversion had flaunted International agreements (Potsdam)

20 November, which happened to be when the seizure took place.[1]

Taking thousands of whales out of the ocean during this final three-year stint must have allowed Roughy populations to burgeon over the following decades.

Toothed Whales New Zealand ○ ○ ○ ○

Around the New Zealand coast, the Soviet fleet [and the Perano Brothers] were hunting sperm whales. They harvested two hundred and forty-eight of them in 1963-1964.

Roughy history - Louisville Ridge ○ ○ ○ ○

The Soviet fleet began fishing the New Zealand Roughy stocks in the eighties, and we obtained translated copies of their reports of the Louisville Ridge. The reports were extensive and so was the title: *"General Physical Geographical Description of the Southern Pacific Seabed - Commercial Fishing Lots at Underwater Mountains 1982-1990"*.

The Soviet ships visiting Louisville had little impact on the region because they only sampled the flat areas. When the Kiwi fishermen started working on the features and edges, the real harvest happened. The opening up of the Ridge meant the `best Kiwi roughy hunters in the world` had first drive over the grounds.

For two years, the hunters searched the Ridges` features, each in their own particular and peculiar way. They searched systematically but weren't afraid to follow a hunch. Every fisherman was aware of each other's fish-finding blind spots and this helped them to be successful. They were accompanied

---

[1] Onassis sold the whaling fleet to the Japanese and that done he promptly founded the anti-whaling trust.

by a posse of mates, who in turn would become skippers in their own right. The factory and deck crew could work hard for days on end if the word 'bonus' was mentioned. There were seafarers out there that were close to the peak of their powers, be it catching or processing, their natural ability was honed on the sea-margins of mainland New Zealand.

The middle areas of the Ridge got special attention from an expert group of 'ice-boat' skippers. They concentrated on the same 40°s latitudes they had worked around coastal New Zealand. They delivered fresh fish instead of frozen product, which meant the seamounts from 39° south; Johnnies, The Pins, Valerie Guyot, and Capetown got continuous all-year attention for three years. These middle seamounts are still producing a load [for an iceboat] a decade later, and are spawning as strong as they ever did.

Thirty-eight-thirty Seamount - [2004] ○ ○ ○ ○

San Liberatore started its 2004 season at the 38°30s seamount; where they had record catches the year before. There was an eagerness to get there, and the effects of mass-impatience saw three boats get there before us. We soon found out arrival times didn't matter because there were poor volumes of fish there in 2004.

Thirty-eight-thirty had almost 600 square sea miles of surface at target depth and it had taken two full years to find where the Roughy spawned - it would take another five years to find the major spawn area. Aussie[1] found the fish in 1996. Dave Cunliffe, who was his co-skipper, said it was a fluke. The larger than life Tasmanian found them at a depth of 742 metres [considered shallow for the latitudes].

---

[1] Greg Clifford Died 2007.(leukaemia)

During the initial plunder of the Ridge, only the spawn spots at The Pins, 43°30s and the 45°s seamounts had been discovered in the first year probably because small seamounts are easier to search.

The decade season at the Ridge was interrupted when our management sent us chasing `radio fish`[1] in the Tasman Sea. It was a full-pitch and expensive seven-day round trip [staying outside the NZ EEZ zone]. Two thousand sea miles for a NIL catch result.

We got back to the Louisville and it was reported we hadn`t missed a thing. We went down the Ridge leap frogging Hori on Amaltal Endeavour. It was the first time in seven years two big boats had gone down the Ridge. It was only the second time *Endeavour* had been to the ridge and the trips were nine years apart.

The point of interest was small Orange Roughy had started to show up in our nets. Some fishermen predicted [without certainty] this would happen. The small fish were around 150mm in length and had ripening roes. They started appearing in the catch as soon as a mark was under pressure. There had been no small fish at the Louisville Ridge before this. You could presume these small fish were recruits and balanced the food supply.

Much has been written about the age of Roughy. Small Roughy showing up in our trawls were ready to drop eggs, which meant they were between twenty and thirty years old [depending on the maths and the expert].

---

[1] Radio fish are the equivalent of wild geese when it`s about chasing.

Roughy age is a disputed subject. It is said Roughy are a long-lived fish. All large Roughy are old and female. It is easy to see age in their heads, and their slime cavities take on a weathered look that is different from the smooth heads of the spawning school fish. An alarmist website has Roughy living *'generally a hundred and fifty years'*. Nothing lives *generally* for a hundred and fifty years in the ocean.

Old fish are eaten by predators. It is all about fitness, and nature has created the likes of the parasites [lice, barnacles, and worms] to deal with age.

100 years old and still gorgeous!

Poster of a school roughy showing limited cavity development.

I saw only one very old fish in ten years of Roughy fishing. Its slime cavities were like craters; its dorsal-spikes were like polished ivory; and its fins had weathered edges. Basil[1] [the Baader man] held it up and exclaimed 'look at this one!' He put it aside for those who wanted to gawk at it, but the old fish

---

[1] Basil Lee ;(Dunedin) Drowned 2010 Tasmania

lost its head the first time Basil was held up by the pound-kicker.

Over a decade, [starting from a virgin stock and with 40,000 tonnes of fish caught], the whole catch, except for one fish, had been school fish. Old fish are unlucky to be caught. They work different currents to the 'schoolies' and usually inhabit slimed-out lairs close to a food source. If you are an old fish on a ridge [or a reef], there is bound to be a competitor who wants your feeding spot and home.

Aside about Fish Age o o o o

The internet has a Goldfish called Goldie that lived until 45 years in Devon. There is a Lungfish named Grandad that is 80 years ancient and lives in Chicago [but was born in Australia]; and the oldest fish and chip shop in the world is in England and is a hundred and sixty years old.at it coincided with the advent of fish trawling.

After Roughy spawn, the females become very emaciated. Their flesh is watery and muscle-less. Their skin has a lifeless colour.

It is obvious these fish will never spawn again [but they earned the same export dollar]. There is no way the spent fish could compete for food. You would expect their place would be taken up by recruits.

What became obvious over a decade at the Louisville was Roughy don't spawn every year and not every spawn involves all the fish. Often schools of males never got to ejaculation stage although they were only a step away.

***

Our decade season continued. The two big boats were working seamounts that had been trawler-free for a few years. There was no need for the two boats to compete at the same seamounts and both the big boats finished the season with success and loads of three hundred tonnes.

Louisville Ridge - August - [2004]

Our boss said he wasn't complaining about the catch but..., he was sending us out to 'the Ridge' again. We were directed to catch a sample load of '*Louisville whitebait*' at the 42°47s 161°56w hill which was covered with the baitfish. The baitfish were Big-eye Cardinalfish and the massive presence of the Cardinals had suggested 'The Vatican' for the seamounts moniker.

One thing was sure; they looked like a baitfish. There are schools of these fish at most of the seamounts from 38°s southwards but *Vatican* is covered with them. They had the strange habit of being head first down the Roughy gullets in the days leading up to a full moon and tail first after the moon. Small observations like that can amuse when you spend long hours at a gutting table. When the cooks fried up a feed of the Cardinals were tasty eating

Big Eye Cardinalfish 12cm average

. *Our management were hoping they might be useable as a bait [or feed] for the big Tunas living at the South Australian gulfs and Tuna farms but it didn't eventuate because the*

Cardinalfish had very high oil content which made them hard to process and store.

When we had caught five tonnes of the Cardinalfish, we were directed to try our luck at the bottom Louisville seamounts for Roughy and it was planned we should try to make up a load with Smooth and Spiky Dory.

Both Dory are low value and present problems. The Spikys stop belts from moving, puncture gloves and fingers, and blunt saw-blades. Smoothys fill the boat with an ammonia smell which gives birth to nose-clogging bogeys. The bogeys look like wriggly white-grubs and they are impossible to dislodge from the fingers and thumbs.

Spiky Dory   2kg Large   Smooth Dory   5Kg Large

The southern Louisville Ridge wears the worst of the Antarctic out-flowing. When the weather is stormy, at least once in an eight-hour shift, an over-sized wave speeds through the area, pushing a boat off course, and leaving the watch keeper in awe. The ferocity of the southern storms make it is hard to fish. The sea slows the boat-speed below the four knots needed to keep the doors spread [and upright] and maintain movement trawl over the sea floor.

We fished the seamounts out to 140° west and down to 55° south. If tonnage was the only criteria for success in the fishing industry, then our out-of-season trip to the bottom of the Louisville was a success.

We caught a Great White Shark at 50° south; its luck run out when it swum into the net while we were hauling. The Great White was small but in prime condition [around 40 kg[1]] with a barrel body that was probably fattened from feasting on plump sea birds and stripling seals. The Indonesians butchered it up, there was no time to get a camera, [and a very fast shutter speed would have been needed if the camera had been on hand]. They did it with obvious pleasure. Ramadan was starting and the shark was a good omen.

Ramadan started when we set sail back to NZ. Our westward course to Wellington [1800 nautical miles away] made the sunset time later by an hour each day. The ever-changing sundown led to a display of patient behaviour from the Muslim devotees. They sat chatting in groups waiting to eat. The chain-smokers amongst them paced the deck, waiting for both sundown and opportunity to have a drag.

We landed 300 tonne of Dory product. The boss said he wasn't complaining but.... He was planning to send us across the Pacific. We asked how far and he replied, "The whole way."

Surge Report - May [2004] ○ ○ ○ ○

Surge reported he was catching Congers again. His nephew [Tai] was back on the coast helping but a little leery about handling the eels. He said there'd been no progress with the quota allocation and sounded sanguine when he noted, 'it's only been in the pipeline for ten years'.

Surge was happy with his Conger catch and said he had twenty [family-size] in the holding cage. He was feeding them dog-roll and he was supplementing the diet with Spotties, When he used the word supplementing, I knew he wasn't far

---

[1] Great Whites are 30 Kg at birth with a dozen in a litter.

from adding antibiotics and vitamins to their feast and he would require restraint when he suggested deer velvet.

"They look to be putting on weight," Surge said about his catch. He had been closely watching the Congers at feeding time and had a behaviour report on the dominant fish. *'Missus two-for-me'* he liked to call her and he shared stories about Conger greed, dominance, and shyness.

"I reckon they are tame enough to spoon feed. You could measure weight gain outcomes, "I could to do a conger feeding thing for the tourists, people like watching eels feeding."

He paused for a moment and said, "And Tai could show the punters how angry he can make them. There may be a market there too, doing conger cage-fighting shows. People will watch anything fighting in a cage."

There was no doubt Surge was an enterpriser.

LOUISVILLE RIDGE

Catch History. Greenweight [Source NIWA]

Year	NORTH ZONE	SOUTH ZONE	VESSELS	CATCH TONNES
1990	34	0	1	34
1991	0	0	NIL	0
1992	28	0	1	28
1993	156	3	2	159
1994	8356	1856	7	10212
1995	5884	2703	31	8587
1996	1536	1682	26	3218
1997	793	701	16	1494
1998	428	2357	13	2783
1999	578	798	17	1376
2000	1116	491	12	1607
2001	645	337	11	982
2002	888	407	15	1203
2003	714	700	11	1414
2004	213	680	12	893
				39100

Vessels that fished the Louisville Ridge [alphabetical order]
Amaltal Endeavor Amaltal Explorer: Amaltal Mariner Amaltal
Voyager: Arrow: Atlantic Elizabeth: Austral Leader: Baldur:
Belinda: Cedric Albert, Clarabelle: Corvina: Derwent
Enterprise: Geng Hai: Dong Wons [various]: Giljannes:
Hopnes: Kap Favel: Kermadec: Komtek: Kursa: Mary Anne:
Nan Hai: Newfoundland Lynx: Ocean Fresh: Ocean Ranger:
Ocean Reward, Osha: Srixon Onward, Oyangs [various]:
Pacific Bounty: Perseverance: Petersen: Rover: San Liberatore:
Saint Giuseppe: Saint Pierre: Santa Monica: San Rangitoto:
Sapun Gora: Seafire: Seamount Explorer: Tasman Viking:
Thomas Harrison: Waipori: Western Ranger: Whitby: Will
Watch and Xing Xing Hai   Source ~Shane .Shore

THE OVERSEA ENDING....

12...The Pae Kiri Kiri Project.

Wellington - November - [2005] ₀ ₀ ₀ ₀

The Indonesian crew were enjoying their time ashore. They had beaming smiles and there was a skip in every step when they used the gangway. Puchani [the bosun] said fresh spring onions and the crisp radishes had perked them up.

Our management were looking glum. They were crying poormouth, and they were eating meals on the boat suggesting there was probably some truth in it. They were trying to sell the Dory catch from the vessel rather than put it into freezer storage, but sales were slow. The three hundred tonnes of Dory product had become their headache and it had shut down any small talk.

After two months in port, only a small part of the Dory catch had been unloaded and serious grumpiness was setting in. The situation was grim; we were being reminded of it every day – it was the fishmonger's way. When share-fishermen feel insecure, they are more likely to accept a smaller share. When the fishmongers try to balance their books, the shortfall comes from the crews' catch-share. Its standard business practice when fish are hard to sell and everyone on board had the *unit standard* for shrinking pay dreams.

***

Surge Separated - September [2005] ○ ○ ○ ○

Surge was single again. His wife [Sue] had absconded while she was visiting her daughter in Australia. When he talked about it, I felt happy my sea-life had saved me from the relationship problems he'd suffered over the years.

I suffered during his past separations. There were times when a month ashore resulted in a month of listening to his 'split-up' agonies. Sue had been telling Surge to change his ways, for a long time, but Surge hadn't listened.

"There's nothing like a divorce to get a fishing-bone itchy," Surge said, then related how he was *at the throats of the Fisheries Ministry* and how he'd managed to get the direct phone-line of a mid-level manager.

He said the manager, 'Sounded like he was deep in the demountable partitioning and probably in a corner office'. Surge had learnt that in October 2007 Congers eels would be officially added to the Quota Management system.

Surge rambled on about fish and quota. He went on, *infinite ad nauseam,* [and add a bit of *ad tedium* too], but before long he returned to the divorce,

"If she thinks she can get me to Australia, she's wrong." None of it surprised me. He needed to talk, although sharing his domestic agonies for the umpteenth time was a test of our friendship.

His next statement was unexpected, "You know how I have been feeding Spotties to the Congers. Well it got me thinking. How about we try to lease some wharf under-water space and farm Spotties. If air-space can be leased then we must be able to lease under-wharf space."

I could hear my mind click into the gear which synchronized with his dream. I had taken the bait and I heard the word 'we'.

He added facts and codicils. "Did you know there's a fifty-million dollar dried-fish market in the Philippines?"

"We could salt the Spotties when the weather is bad. Did you know there's a thirty-million dollar market in salt dried fish in the Balkans? What about we use flavoured salt, nobody uses the tasty salts like, Szechuan pepper-salt or sage salt, we could start a new taste sensation."

"What about we smoke the spotties, everybody knows New Zealand has the best woods for smoking things - everyone loves smoked fish. What about we do barbeque packs?"

He had reached the `what about` stage of a new fishing adventure.

When I told Surge, my boat was going to scout the South Pacific he said, "You'll be gone for months. by the time you get back, I'll have a wharf and permits." His mind was in dream gear and I expected nothing less.

"We could probably turn it into a tourist business – tours of the breeding pens or the stockholds and visitors could catch their own fish with hired rods and jigs. We could have a smoked-fish shop with fresh-baked bread."

"They have been catching a fish in the Sea of Galilee since before BC that looks like a Spotty," he said with authority.

"Spotties could be the same but we would need a name change for the marketing bit. The fish in the Galilee Sea is called St Peter's fish." He was talking with pauses and spoon-feeding me his drift,

"The spot, on the side of the fish, is said to be St Peter's thumb mark and we could market them with a coin in their mouths like the fish Peter caught to pay the taxes."

"The Bay of Islands would be the perfect place, there's a lot to do – I'll keep you in the loop." When Surged dreamed, he did it at pace, in fact, dreaming was the only thing he did with speed. The phone went dead, he didn`t say good-bye [or over], later his first email arrived...

Spotted wrasse

New Zealand Spotty

Like most wrasses this species is a protogynous hermaphrodite - each individual begins life as a female and later changes sex to become a male. The larvae drift in the plankton for about 2 months before settling as tiny juveniles 15 to 20 millimetres long, in the fronds of the common kelp 'Ecklonia radiata'. These exclusively female young fish grow rapidly and reach maturity in September when about 12 centimetres long. After 1 or 2 years they change sex to become males.   Spotties are commonly caught by young anglers off harbour wharves and rocks.

Maori name; Pae Kiri Kiri

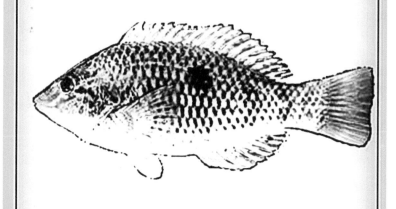

East Pacific Ridge - January [2006] ○ ○ ○ ○

The *San Lib* was ready to sail. Our pay was put on hold and the Dory fish had been put into cold storage [reluctantly]. The vessel's bridge electronics had a new computer with a program for 3D seafloor mapping. The new electronics produced predictive realistic seabed-scapes and they updated in real time.

The program [Piscatus] had a database of the planet's ocean-floor; it was derived from sea-surface levels, micro-measured from satellites.[1] It was the same electronic tool needed to fly inter-continental missiles. 3D graphics required two flat screens and they took up the last of the free space surrounding the fishing station area in the wheelhouse.

New computer programs produce new stuff ups [and this one was no different], but when it worked properly, the mapping program was very accurate.

We started across the Pacific looking for fish at the seamounts where we knew no NZ boats had searched. To our knowledge, there had been only three Pacific Ocean searches before us and their efforts went unrewarded. Earlier expeditions were unsuccessful, but there was a seamount `half way to Chile` where the previous expeditions had managed to score a few Roughy. The seamount was 3450 sea miles from New Zealand and we would search all the seamounts on the way to it, using our new 3D mapping capabilities.

The plan was to search the seamounts on the way to the East Pacific Rise and finish up at the Nazca Ridge. We discovered the first part of the Pacific was full of Guyots [table-mountains] and none of them had signs of life.

---

[1] The sea surface level is higher where the ocean pushes (propelled by Coriolis forces) over subterranean structures (mountains & pinnacles)

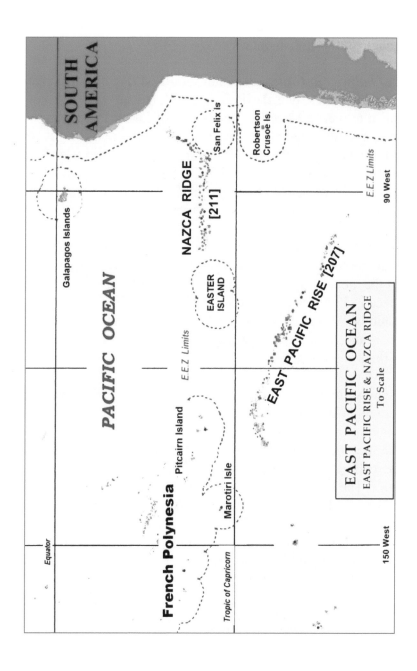

We 'hill-hopped' on a very flat sea, it seemed to go on forever, no clouds, no breeze, no waves and the only movement was a straggle of flying fish once a day.

The `halfway to Chile` seamount produced five oldish fish and they didn`t look like the Roughy we knew so well. We set a course to the East Pacific Rise [south of Easter Island] and we navigated the vessel to get prime time coverage at the seamounts. The East Rise is a large area to search and our searching quickly degenerated into drive-overs.

After six weeks of searching the East Rise for small returns and little sign of life, our management ordered us north to the Nazca Ridge.

The *Nazca* lies in International waters off Peru. Nobody on board complained about management's decision even though it left the most likely seamounts on the East Rise unsounded. The Nazca is 5300 sea miles from New Zealand. Our target species would be Alfonsino, a fish used in banquets and ceremonies in Japan and they were returning good prices on the world fish markets at the time.

When we arrived at the first of the Alfonsino seamounts there were light-buoys blinking all over the place. The area was twinkling and the lights marked Langoustine[1] pots. It didn't take long before a langoustine boat appeared on our radar and was calling us up on the VHF radio. "Were we going to set pots?" The boats skipper asked in a heavy Latin accent.

We told him we were a trawler looking for Alfonsino fish and we were going to work well clear of his pots. Something got lost in translation and it put him out of countenance. His accent got heavier, his tone less friendly and he began pleading for time to remove his pots.

---

[1] Called Scampi in New Zealand.

Langoustine pots are made with two metal hoops [metre diameter] covered with light-gauge meshed netting, like a bag net or fyke. The pots are collapsible for storage and a typical langoustine boat uses 2000 pots strung along eight lines.

In a normal season, the scampi boats lose a quarter of the pots [500]. With a trawler working the area, there was a good chance they would lose the two thousand in a night.

On the high seas, 'might is right' and it is something pot and line fisherman are well aware of. The same rule applies to trawlers, but in that case, it is a matter of horsepower and wire diameter.

We had told the Langoustine boat we would be trawling on the other side of the seamount from his pots, but he spent the next six hours lifting his gear and he thanked us when he left.

We started catching Alfonsino from the first tow and the factory started processing thirty tonnes of product on a daily basis.

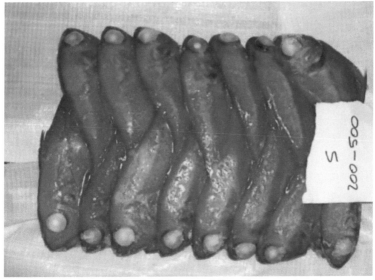

A glazed block of frozen Alfonsino product

The fish hold was filling up steadily but it became obvious the job would take more time than had been estimated and we would get short of fuel and food. The Indonesian crew were fretting because there was only four tonne of rice left on-board.

Their leaders feared a breakdown of morale and a meeting was set up with a supply-ship servicing a squid fleet, working a couple of hundred miles to the north of us.

We arrived at the transfer position at nigh-ttime and the squid fleet was hard at it. A squid fleet the size of the one we encountered should have lit up the night-sky for miles [and been seen from deep outer space], but this fleet was made up of old boats with poor lighting.

There were more than a hundred of them and the fleet was `assorted craft, type: hulks` from the dingy school of squid jigging. A few of the vessels had automated jiggers, but on the others, hand-lines were used from the first main deck.

The water was black with squid-ink and it was an odd sight on a half-moon night. Our Indonesian crew started fishing with handmade lures. There was skill and excitement on display as they plucked the squid out of the inky water.

Our fish sounder was showing surface-to-seafloor life and the new 3D computer mapping system was out of control despite the gain being set 'close to zero'.

Just before dawn, we hooked up a towrope and fuel pipe to the tanker and then pumped fuel while the tanker towed us around on a flat black-sea. The tankers workboat delivered two tonne of rice. The Indonesian crew complained the newly delivered grain wasn't the grain they liked … but then they said it was good with fresh Squid.

Orders arrived from New Zealand for the boat to return home. The trip back to New Zealand allowed us to scout seamounts which hadn't been sounded on the way to the Nazca. When we docked in NZ, we were told the money earned from the

Alfonsino had barely covered the costs of the expedition. Pay insecurity attacks were starting again. The boss said he wasn't complaining but ...he hoped the next Louisville season would be a good one.

Pae Kiri Kiri Project - April [2006] ○ ○ ○ ○

Surge arrived at the boat and he was heeled over by an old leather briefcase. The case was a relic, it concertina'd open when the locking-clasp was slipped and it was obvious there would be problems getting the paperwork back into it. I twigged he was going to push the contents onto me. The first documents he dealt my way were about fish dehydrators. There were multitudes of dehydrators. Surge liked the ones that used some of the leached fish-oil to run a small circulating fan driven by a lighted wick. I was intrigued by the ingenuity and the size of the fish roe dryers.

He told how he had used ranch-slider doors for a test dryer, "I laid them down propped on bricks and put the Spotties on the insect-screen between the glass doors. It worked good, twenty kilos of dried Spotty in four days just like that - tommy!" When Surge finished a statement with the word 'tommy' it indicated it was a fact and could be considered a miracle.

"Everyone likes the dried fish," Surge spruiked, "There's probably a market in New Zealand."
I wondered about quality, picturing the fish laid out drying where bush-flies had loitered.

"I've adapted a conger pot to catch the Spotties," he was anxious to get the details out, "We don't need to worry about a wharf unless we run with a tourist option - I think we're onto a winner this time." He sounded sure about it but I'd heard his 'onto a winner' statement so many times before.

"Did you gut the Spotties?" I asked, bothered by the detail, but he wasn't listening. He pulled more documents out of the old briefcase: brochures on vacuum packing, bar codes, salting techniques and Resource Consent applications. They started to pile high as he explained the schemes progress. I was starting to feel like I was part of the project and there was no way out.

Our discussions went until the early morning hours. We were still mulling over the possibilities when the Kiwi crew got back to the vessel and interrupted us with high tales in slurred English.

Louisville Ridge - [2006] o o o o

The 2006 Louisville Roughy season began with small bags of fish which became larger as the season progressed. By the end of June, we caught a hundred-tonne more than the same period the year before. It was only a statistic but it made everyone happy.

In July, we lost a full set of fishing gear and worse, we lost over a thousand metres of trawl-wire. We had spare nets and doors, but not enough wire to tow them. The lost trawl came fast on a slope with no obvious hook ups, and the gear loss made us return to New Zealand.

Our departure from the grounds coincided with the arrival of a violent storm-front that hastened our passage and stopped any fishing on the ridge while we away. In port, we were reminded the Dory was still selling slowly and the price of the lost-gear replacement was going to come out of the catch share.

We were back at the Ridge in just over a week. We cruised down the spawn spots catching factory-friendly bags of fish at all the seamounts. Factory-friendly bags are those that come on deck just as the factory is doing a clean-up from the last catch. Typically, the bags are more than a full pound load and allow for an easy freezer operation.

It was great fishing, almost cruise-control stuff. We arrived at a seamount, spent four or five hours looking and then harvested fifty tonne of fish out of a mark before moving on for a repeat performance a couple of hundred miles further south.

We had a collective smugness because we had high expectations for the 47°s seamounts. We'd enjoyed success there before and we knew there was a good body of fish there and no opposition boats.

When we arrived at the 47°s seamount, we started trawling a mark that formed for an hour in the early morning hours. Paul [Hendry] our skipper was in an inventive mood and tried a risky trawl shot. The boat was a net down that year, but a net down has never stopped any roughy hunter with a mark to shoot, even if he had to dig the school out of a narrow gully.

As soon as the net landed, we were catching fish and the net monitor was showing fish marks from ground-line to headline.

When we started hauling the gear in, the pressure gauges indicated a good catch. It wasn't long before the wire began thudding onto the trawl drums causing sparks, to shoot into the night air like tracer bullets.

The forces vibrated the vessel started alerting the on-shift crew and waking up the off-shift crew. Within minutes, smiling faces started appearing at all the trawl-deck doors.

Bringing big bags on-board is a nervy time and everyone was remarking how good it was to have the new trawl wire. Getting big bags to the surface requires concentration and care. The ships heaving can snap wire in an instant. A slow speed is needed with a course to counteract the effects of the waves, wind and swell and often side on is best.

A large bag is only considered safely landed when the big strops are wrapped around the double-mesh and it has been dragged up the deck by the bull winch. There is always a bit of fish damage getting the last cod ends on board, but we had few problems decking the catch and its size had `packed it down`.

Jason the winch driver said his knees had turned to jelly and his heart was thumping when we started back tipping the catch into the pound.

Time to take another bite with the Bull-wire [two cod ends hanging over the stern]

Two days later George [Baranski], the factory manager, reported the catch had been one hundred and fifty tonnes. It was the biggest bag of fish any of us had seen in eleven years fishing at the Ridge. The big bag of fish was the final act for the season and it dominated all conversation.

When we docked, everyone wanted to see the photos and hear all about it. We dined out on it and the fare was excellent. The boss considered the season successful but once again, he said "I'm not complaining but ... I want the boat to go to the North Atlantic."

The Mid Atlantic Rise was mentioned along with Morocco. *Morocco hit me like a kick in the Timbuktu's'*, as they are likely to say in Jackson Bay. It gave my mind a jolt. Somehow, Morocco and adventure are closely linked in my brain.

The voyage to the North Atlantic would be our third crossing of the Pacific for the year. Those who hated sea travel without any fishing were groaning.

The knowledgeable on board were saying the Panama Canal was 'seething hot' at Christmas time and how there was a three-day wait in Balboa before the transit of the canal. Those experienced in the canals operations told how waiting at anchor for the passage sucked up the heat and turned the boat into oven. The word seething had hit my cautionary nerve, but I signed on. Morocco was an opportunity I couldn't resist.

Wellington - July [2006] ○ ○ ○ ○

We sailed from Wellington in November and the skipper [Paul Hendry] entered an order in the Bridge Log reading '*Straight to Hamilton Island'*. It was a little bit of humour, because Hamilton Island [named by Kung Wilson] had never produced more than a tonne of fish over the decade we worked the Ridge. There was a rumour one other boat had steamed straight to it.

The Hamilton Island seamount is 598 meters deep at its shallowest part. On the Ridge, Hamilton is a good depth for baitfish and it has some very likely Roughy ground but it has never shown any fish sign. It seems in a zone of its own.

There were no fish marks at Hamilton Island and thinking there might be was extreme optimism. Deflated extreme-optimism is easy to swallow and we were `out of there`.

Our propeller pitch was increased to the max and the main-engines were asked for full power. You could feel the machinery balance as the two big engines took over. The bow lifted, the pyros started rising, drawers and cupboard doors rattled to the beat of the boat and we left the Louisville Ridge at full steaming speed.

Our course was set to cross the Pacific to the Panama Canal. Leaving the Louisville Ridge seemed a long good-bye. We had just caught the ridge's biggest bag of fish and it was hard to think we might never be back there. Sea plots were filed and large ocean-scale charts started covering the chart table, while the new 3D electronics blinked 'RENDERING' in red LED lettering.

The Louisville Ridge had been a seasonal hunt for New Zealand fishermen for over a decade. The fishery had been predicted to collapse in quick time but fish are still being caught in good quantities.

The big companies [Sanford and Sealord] had sent vessels out to the Ridge and some of the smaller players in the New Zealand fishing industry like Chris Robinson [Giljannes, Pacific Bounty] were involved with more than one vessel. However, by 2005, only one small concern was out there. It was the Brays [son and father or vice versa], with their vessel *Waipori*.

At various times, the Louisville Ridge had attracted all the prominent New Zealand fishing names: Lim, Talley, Muollo, Vella, Simunovitch, Barbarich, Vinnaccia and Kotzikas families had all gambled on a catch at the ridge.

The Lims and the Muollo/Vinnaccia combination had each sent seven different boats to the Ridge. Some seasons they had three boats at the Ridge at one time.

While *San Liberatore* was steaming away, I wondered if I would be back to fish the Ridge again, instinct told me the Panama and beyond, was a one-way trip for the ship.

I had nine good years out of eleven at the Louisville Ridge and in the fishing world, that's a good statistic.

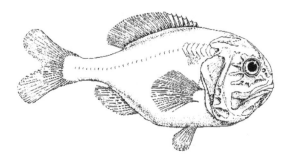

"Whoever the last fisherman turns out to be, it is certain that he will be fishing for an Orange Roughy"
........Such is the habitat and habits of the Roughy fish

Postscript - 2014

The Louisville Ridge was a deep-sea fisher's dream; it was big and untouched. It was remote with innumerable seamounts at Roughy target-depth.

The Ridge continues to produce a thousand tonnes of fish a year. New laws have now been passed regulating the Louisville fishery for vessels working out of New Zealand. The laws are not *'too little too late'* but a timely act which should balance the fishery, but its remoteness will always be the best barrier to over-exploitation.

The Talley and Muollo families have continued fishing the Louisville Ridge to this day. They have the boats for it [*Amaltal Mariner, Amaltal Apollo , Voyager*] and presumably a love of the fishery.

Afterword - 2014

Surge is now a kiwi living in Australia, where he has a good thing going, doing up old caravans. The conger catching gear and quota were sold and his bit of Pakahi out the back of Atarau is still evolving at grow-slow pace. His house is twisting and skewing, but it's no concern because it started contorting soon after he opened the first pack of *'shaky-heart'* from Donaldson's mill.

Surge has a new fish-dream and as usual, he is pumped up when he talks about it. He's moved on from Spotty farming [although he thinks the Intellectual Rights must be worth something]. He has become obsessed with fishing the crabs of The Great Australian Bight, `*out to twenty fathoms*`.

He says, "Crab eaters aren't fussy – as long as there's a picture of a crab on the can – they'll eat it."

"Bight Crabmeat, what do think of the name?"
He has the enthusiasm of a much younger dreamer, still, it's said, 'There's a lot of boy in the fisherman'.

At last contact he had reported [for the first time in his life], "I can bankroll the lot tommy," and as usual he adds, "The project is at the final planning stages. All we need is an old trawler and some crab traps. We'll cover the whole area - Elliston, Eucla, Esperance - 2000 miles of coast, don't you know?"

I heard him say *we* and I wasn't surprised.

It's a big dream to fish *'Nullarbor Beach'*. A friend should have advised him that some scaling down wouldn't hurt, but you can't discourage Surge. He always has a fishing dream and he is dogged in the pursuit of it.

My employment is now seasonal in the seismic search for oil fields. The job makes one of Surge's fishing dreams a more than tempting prospect.

This is a first book. For years, friends and relatives kept saying, *'you should write a book'* and suggestible I am. Others kept asking questions about trawler-fishing deep sea and 'Roughy' is an effort to satisfy their inquisitiveness.

The two-page preface to this book was described as verbose by editors, and they were probably right, but when I made the preface more compendious, I realized they didn't understand the fibre of my yarn.

It took a decade to write about a decade of fishing and in turn, writing became a compulsive pastime.

Nowadays, I am working on the chapters that were jettisoned from this composition. The book will be called, *'Mending a Three Legger'* and it`s about off-season fishing ... and after that, there`s the tale of *Beryl Creek* [which must be told]. 'Beryl' is a fishing tale set in outback Australia

Author: Working on a wing. [photo :Darcy Robinson]

CPSIA information can be obtained
at www.ICGtesting.com
Printed in the USA
LVHW011117300523
748331LV00027BA/87